SCHOLASTIC

50 WRITING ACTIVITIES
for Meeting Higher Standards

MARILYN PRYLE

New York • Toronto • London • Auckland • Sydney
Mexico City • New Delhi • Hong Kong • Buenos Aires

Dedication

for Gavin and Tiernan, the smart, kind, joyful beings I share this life with

Acknowledgments

The meager work of one person reflects the work of many, and I am enormously grateful for the support and effort of others that provide the foundation of this book. As always, I am first indebted to the students who have passed through my classroom and so freely shared their intellect and creativity; most recently those students have been from Abington Heights High School in Clarks Summit, PA. I am grateful as well to the larger community and administration of the Abington Heights School District for their continued support. I am most humbled by and thankful for the help of my colleagues, especially Julie Lartz, Andrea Bartlett, and Rae Rudzinski, for supplying me with ideas, encouragement, and student work. This book is also a result of the support and expertise of many people at Scholastic, including Tara Welty, Maria Chang, Joanna Davis-Swing, and Sarah Morrow. Finally, I would not have the time or space to write anything without my husband Tim: Thank you for giving me a room of my own.

Editor: Joanna Davis-Swing
Cover Designer: Michelle H. Kim
Interior Designer: Sarah Morrow

ISBN: 978-1-338-11145-3
Copyright © 2017 by Marilyn Pryle. All rights reserved.
Published by Scholastic Inc. Printed in the U.S.A.
First printing, June 2017.

2 3 4 5 6 7 8 9 10   40   23 22 21 20 19 18

CONTENTS

Introduction 4

Ways to Use This Book 6

PART 1 ▶ PRACTICES

Powerful Writing Practices 9

1 Life List 9
2 Weak Word Wipeout 10
3 Sentence Mash-Up 12
4 Model Chop 14

5 Intro Intrigue 16
6 Cultivate a Conclusion 18
7 Amp Up the Verbs! 20
8 Editing Check Sheets 22

PART 2 ▶ INDIVIDUAL WRITING ACTIVITIES

Narrative Writing 23

Writing Assignments and Prewriting Sheets

9 Setting Sketch 27
10 Character Sketch 29
11 Free Verse Memory Poem 33
12 Autobiographical Incident 35
13 Proverb Story 40
14 Retelling of a Legend 42

15 Historical Ballad 44
16 Personal Ballad 46
17 Children's Book 48
18 Living Legend 50
19 Short Story 52
20 Historical Fiction 54

Expository Writing 56

Writing Assignments and Prewriting Sheets

21 Introduce Yourself! 60
22 What's in a Name? 61
23 Me, in Metaphors 63
24 Epic Hero Shield and Reflection 65
25 Classify Your Crib 68
26 Process Essay 70
27 Ode 72

28 Thank-You Letter 74
29 Compare and Contrast Essay 76
30 Break Up With a Bad Habit 78
31 School Survival Guide 80
32 News Account 82
33 Passion Pursuit 84
34 Ponder the Progress 86

Persuasive Writing 88

Writing Assignments and Prewriting Sheets

35 Travel Brochure 94
36 Product Review 96
37 Book Review 98
38 Arts Review 100
39 Parental Persuasion 102
40 Letter to the Principal 104
41 Letter for Social Change 106
42 Public Service Announcement 108

43 Personal Essay 110
44 Analysis of a Song 112
45 Analysis of a Poem 114
46 Analysis of Art 116
47 Analysis of a Character 118
48 Analysis of a Short Story 120
49 Analysis of an Article 122
50 Connection Inspection 124

How to Access Online Resources 127

Introduction

I've dreamed of this book for a long time. Although I've written several books in the past about the nature of writing workshop, I know from experience as a classroom teacher that some of the most valuable resources are more practical than philosophical. But before we get to the 50 practical exercises in this book, let me root all of it in the philosophical. In my years of teaching writing to students, my convictions about the power of writing and its benefits for students as learners and human beings have only deepened. Despite the shifting requirements and expectations on student writing, despite the debates about the future of written forms, modes, and genres, these are the truths I know about writing:

1. Strong writing is powerful and can be learned.

Although modern-day writing continues to morph into many forms, the written word persists and is more powerful than ever. The strength of a clear, engaging, meaningful message cannot be underestimated. The good news is that with practice, effective writing can be learned. I try to dispel the myth that some people are born talented writers and everyone else is not. I strive to convince students that the stuff of their lives can be a basis for powerful writing, and that they can learn to write well if they commit to it.

2. Writing is an extension of thought, not just a record of it.

The act of writing always yields new insights. Often, we don't know what we thought about a topic until we start writing about it. When students begin to experience this truth they gain confidence and excitement—writing becomes an adventure. The brain and the heart reveal themselves through writing, if we practice. We must show up for it, though: Like a sport or hobby, we must show up for practice. We must be present.

3. Writing helps the writer be present and notice.

As with any task, it is possible to become absorbed when we write and experience full presence. One must turn inward; one must be silent. What a beautiful gift to give to students in a world full of loud, shallow distractions. And writing can give students even more than that—in order to write well in any genre, students must look deeply into their own daily lives and memories, at the colors, smells, and sunlight, at eyes, hands, and words. With practice, this persistent looking can expand into a way of being, a way of living more in the present at all times, a constant noticing. This is the true grace of the writing life. If we can give even a fraction of that to our students through the work of writing practice, we will have succeeded.

4. Writers become better by writing.

A coach would never teach an athlete a technique once or twice and expect her to be able to perform it perfectly from that point on. Free throws, flip turns, serves, and spins are practiced thousands of times each year; so it is with writing. A tweet I quote regularly is Kelly Gallagher's (2013) maxim: "It doesn't matter how good the writing standards are if students aren't writing way more than the teacher can read." A goal of this book is to give teachers plenty of writing to choose from to keep students constantly writing. Although rubrics are included with each activity, don't be intimidated: Do what works for you. Plenty of writing in my class goes formally ungraded but verbally conferenced. It all helps.

5. Writing makes students read like writers.

When students practice real writing in several genres, they begin to read not as passive spectators but as knowledgeable apprentices. They begin to internalize the tenets of strong writing, and they can sense its presence. Instead of simply saying a text is "good" or "bad," they can identify the skills employed or the ones lacking. They learn to read from the inside-out, like writers, simultaneously seeing the finished product and its working parts.

6. Writing as a practice develops one's voice.

Regular writing about one's life, observations, reflections, and opinions leads to a strong sense of voice. The writer comes to realize his unique style and outlook. Ideally, the writer also comes to believe that this individual perspective has value, that he has something to contribute to the world. Though each of us is only one voice, we are all important notes in the chorus of humanity. As educators, we must convince students of this by helping them write about their lives and opinions honestly and clearly, and by encouraging them to participate in the larger conversation of our shared existence.

Ways to Use This Book

The activities presented here can be selected, grouped, modified or expanded to fit into your current curriculum. Regardless of what your course or level is—English Literature, Writing Workshop, or ELL— these lessons should help you get your students writing. You may want to use these activities as classwork, homework, or groupwork; you may want to assign one activity at a time to the class; you may want to present several activities at once and let students choose the ones they're drawn to. If you use my book *Writing Workshop in Middle School,* this book should save you much time in creating assignments and prewriting sheets.

Part 1: Practices consists of ideas that won't produce a polished piece of writing by themselves but may help generate ideas, habits, or fluency that could help with other writing activities. These practices can also be taught and retaught as mini-lessons alongside any individual writing activity. You will notice that the concepts in this section show up on almost every set of directions and every rubric in the Individual Writing Activities section.

Part 2: Individual Writing Activities consists of 42 ready-to-go writing assignments. This section is arranged into three blocks: Narrative, Expository, and Persuasive. I personally have used all of these activities at one point or another, though not all in the same year with the same class. Use the assignments that are most helpful to your students and most applicable to your existing curriculum. Below are some thoughts about how to use these activities.

- **Link to the Standards:** Each block of Individual Activities begins with a list of common standards that are addressed within that block. These standards are paraphrased from the Common Core State Standards but reflect the rigorous standards used by most states and districts. If any additional standard is addressed with a specific writing activity, it is noted in the introduction to that particular activity. All of the practices and writing activities in this book support the common overall standard at right.

> **STANDARD**
> Write regularly throughout the year in several genres, in longer and shorter pieces, for a variety of purposes and audiences.

- **Scaffold the Learning:** Generally, the Individual Writing Activities are arranged to progress in difficulty within each block. For example, it is easier to write a compelling short story after some practice with a character sketch; it is easier to write an analysis of a poem after practicing cohesive paragraphs in an introductory letter. As you choose the activities best suited for your class, always keep scaffolding in mind.

- **Mix and Match Activities:** Even though each block of Individual Writing Activities is scaffolded within itself, it does not mean each block's activities should be done together before moving on to the next block. Mix and match assignments as needed! For example, Introduce Yourself! would make a wonderful assignment for the beginning of the year, followed by some simpler and more personal narrative pieces (such as Setting Sketch or Character Sketch). More expository pieces, such as Process Essay or Compare and Contrast Essay, might help students understand the basics of organization before they try a persuasive piece. You can also give students a choice from several assignments at once. Having a choice from five or six activities will give students a sense of ownership and motivation.

- **Use Mini-Lessons:** Although I do not suggest specific mini-lessons for each writing activity, feel free to accompany the activities with any mini-lessons your class may need. There is a list of some possible mini-lessons online; see page 127 for instructions on how to access. (The topic of mini-lessons is covered extensively in my book *Writing Workshop for Middle School*.) Have students keep a notebook of mini-lessons that they can refer to at any time. You will notice that on the Writing Assignments, strong introductions and conclusions, for example, are consistently required, though not explained each time. If these are taught early on as mini-lessons, students will be able to consult their notes throughout the year for techniques.

FLIP THE MINI-LESSONS
If you record and post your mini-lessons online, students will have access to them all year, whenever they need a topic the most!

- **Employ the Writing Process:** In this book, the writing process follows the same pattern with each of the Individual Writing Activities: reading, prewriting, drafting, revising and editing, and submitting. For some assignments, the Prewriting Sheet is a page; for others, two. Still others ask students to prewrite on a blank sheet. Use these in whatever way is most helpful to you. The Writing Assignments are broken into steps and checkboxes to guide students through the process; use this format to create your own activity sheets for additional or alternate writing assignments.

- **Assign Model Reading:** As you know, writing is inextricably connected to reading. Each written assignment here has an actual model or the idea for a model attached to it, with questions to focus students on important aspects of the genre. Some models are included in the online resources (see pages 127–128); other models would be most effective if written by you; still others should be as current as possible from recent media. (The introductions to the assignments give guidance on this.) In addition, if you can find model reading in your classroom texts, use it. (With the exception of the analyses at the end of the book, these assignments are not specific responses to readings; however, tying your in-class reading to a writing activity will deepen the experience for students.) Finally, as you use these activities, save any student writing which could help other students in the future. Soon you will have your own personal trove of samples.

- **Consider Length Requirements:** You will notice that in the instructions for each Individual Writing Activity, a space is left blank for a minimum length requirement. I have found that setting a minimum length pushes students to keep writing even when they don't want to. (If they repeat or go off-topic, explain this in a conference and tell them to revise.) You can set the lengths to any amount—if you want to do a certain activity but not spend much time on it, set the length to a couple paragraphs or even just a paragraph, depending on your class. If you want an activity to serve as a formal paper or an in-depth project, require it to be longer.

- **Require Titles:** Another requirement for every Individual Writing Activity, regardless of its genre or format, is the inclusion of a title. This is not just a formality; using engaging titles reflects the writer's command of a piece. It demonstrates knowledge and control over what one has created. Crafting effective titles would make a useful mini-lesson at the beginning of the year; use titles of what you're reading in class as examples.

- **Use Rubrics:** Each Writing Assignment in the Individual Writing Activities section ends with a rubric that reflects the specific skills required for that activity, as well as other skills that denote strong writing. I like having the rubric right below the directions because it makes the Writing Assignment like a contract students can see up front. Regardless of the assignment, all skills are divided into the same five categories: Structure, Process, Ideas, Language, and Grammar/Spelling. These categories have worked best in my classes; however, as with all parts of this book, tailor the rubric to best suit your students.

- **Invite Revision:** As you know, revision within the writing process cannot be emphasized enough! In my other books, especially *Writing Workshop for Middle School* and *Purposeful Conferences, Powerful Writing!*, I've written extensively about conferencing with students and helping them revise. Although conferencing techniques are beyond the focus of this book, notice that each rubric contains a column for a Preliminary Grade and a Revised Grade. I let students revise for *full points back*; in fact, I expect them to. **Use grading not as a punishment for failed attempts, but as a way to reward efforts at revision and emphasize its importance in the writing process.**

- **Encourage Editing:** Several editing check sheets are included in the online resources; see pages 22 and 127–128. Students should get in the habit of self-editing all the time, but peer editing will also build their eye for revision. You may want to alternate between one or both types of editing for different assignments. Or, you may want them to self- and peer-edit each time, depending on your students and time constraints.

- **Differentiate Assignments:** These assignments are, in a way, automatically differentiated, since you can use the rubric to best serve each student. You can vary the length requirements; you can narrow or broaden the definition of each skill; you can base grades off certain sections of writing. For example, a struggling ELL student might have the Grammar/Spelling grade based on only the first paragraph or on a single grammatical pattern. The one area you may have to adjust is model writing; only one piece of model writing per activity is included for each assignment. To have more advanced or less complicated pieces, you must find or create them. To further differentiate the activities, use the pattern of the Writing Assignments presented here to construct your own adjusted versions.

• • •

Whatever parts of this book you use, it is my sincere hope that these activities help your students as writers, readers, and thinkers. I hope that by the end of the year in your class, they are able to look a bit more closely at their worlds. I hope they are not afraid to face a blank page or seek out a better word, and I hope they believe that they have something to say and ways to say it. Enjoy this journey.

Powerful Writing Practices

1 Life List

Many of the ideas in this book require students to write from their own lives, using their experience and prior knowledge as fodder for the assignment. Even as adolescents, students have a rich wealth of lived experience to write about, but few of them believe that they do. If I ask them what makes a "good writer," they will say it is someone with an extraordinary and exciting life. They subscribe to the myth that since they are young (or middle/upper/lower class, or smart/not smart), they have nothing interesting or important to write. However, this is of course untrue. Good writing comes from our own lives—the sights, sounds, smells, people, memories, and feelings we all have swirling around in our minds and hearts. To write something meaningful, one does not have to have lived an "extraordinary" life; one only must look closely at the life she has. And age is irrelevant—as Willa Cather said, "Most of the basic material a writer works with is acquired before the age of fifteen." All year, my mantra is: "You have something to write. Your own life is profoundly interesting, if you look closely enough." The first step I take to prove this to them is to have them construct a "Life List." Students do this in the front of their English notebooks, so they can refer to it all year. No one will be able to declare, "I have nothing to write." Take about a day or two to set this up, asking questions from the Life List Questions sheet (Resource 1; see right) and giving students time in between each question to write silently. They do not need to write sentences; they can write a list of words or phrases. There are no wrong answers, and no one need understand the list but they.

When students are finished, most will have two pages or more. Emphasize to them that this is the stuff of their lives that would make for interesting writing. They alone are the experts of these lists, and they should add to their lists as any new ideas pop into their heads. Tell students to look over their lists and feel proud of what they know.

CONNECT
Write your own Life List and share it with students as you read the questions. This might help jog their memories for something in their own lives to add.

Life List Questions

(Read slowly and give students time to write.)

1. Who are some important people in your life? Name them specifically. Family, friends? How about pets? (Individuals can be living or deceased.)
2. Who are some interesting people in your life? They could be people you are close to, or people who are interesting acquaintances, like the guy across the street who sings a song called "Mr. Pancake" to the tune of "Mr. Sandman" to call his dog home. What makes them interesting?
3. What are some of your favorite places? Name them. Think of indoors; think of outdoors. Add a few details if they come to mind. What are some interesting places you've seen, even if you didn't like them? What are some places you hate?
4. What are some of your favorite belongings, things that mean a lot to you? Some jewelry? A necklace, watch, bracelet, ring? Something in your room? A piece of clothing?
5. What are some of your favorite movies? What are some movies you didn't like? Do you have a favorite play?
6. What are some of your favorite books? Favorite short stories? (It may help to name some from the previous years' curriculums.) Favorite poems?
7. Who is your favorite band or singer? Whom do you dislike?
8. What in the school would you change, if you could? What do you wish your school had?
9. What would you change in your town? What do you wish your town had? What do you wish your town didn't have?
10. What in our country would you change? Any laws or policies? Should any laws be added?
11. What makes you angry or annoyed?
12. What are your hobbies? What are things you know how to do well?
13. What else are you good at? What else do you know about, even if you think it's no big deal—like delivering papers, or babysitting, or playing card games?
14. At home, what do you know a lot about?
15. In school, what are your favorite subjects? What subjects are easiest for you?
16. Can you remember any dreams that you've had that stand out in your mind? What happened?
17. Do you ever daydream? In the car, in school, or somewhere else? What do you think about?
18. Try to remember a time in your life that was sad. Write a phrase or two. If you have more than one example, write both.
19. Try to remember a time that was scary. Write a phrase or two.
20. Try to remember a time that was difficult, or a time when you had to meet a big challenge.
21. Note a time in your life that was funny—it could be with your family or friends. Maybe you have a few examples. Jot down a phrase for each.
22. Think of a time that was really joyful or happy. Maybe you can think of two or three times.

50 Writing Activities for Meeting Higher Standards by Marilyn Pryle

The Life List Questions sheet is available as Resource 1 online; see page 127 for instructions on how to access.

2 Weak Word Wipeout

Part I: Ban Weak Words

This practice is a year-long commitment: Banish weak words from the classroom. Outlaw the use of words such as *good, great, bad, cool, things, stuff, awesome, sort of,* and *kind of* for the year, at least in students' writing. To illustrate the effectiveness of using stronger, more specific words, do a mini-lesson at the beginning of the year. Then hold students responsible for the skill all year; they'll never be able to use a weak word again without thinking twice! (You will notice that "no banned words" appears as a criterion on every rubric in the book.)

1. Ask students to jot down a movie or television episode they've seen recently that they thought was "great." Tell them to write a sentence saying the movie or episode "was great."

2. Below the sentence, have them list all the reasons it was great. They should try to think of at least five reasons. (You might have to help them with questions: How was the acting? The plot? The music? Was the movie scary, thrilling, inspiring, moving? How would you describe the scenery?)

3. Have them look at their lists. Tell them to change any words like *good, excellent,* or *terrific* to more specific words. (Again, you might have to help with suggestions: Was the acting *convincing*? Was the plot *exciting*? Was the message *joyful*? Was the scenery *beautiful*?)

4. Under the list, have them construct a full sentence with the movie or TV show title and their top three reasons in it, avoiding the word *great* or any other weak words. Have volunteers share their sentences.

5. Make a point to explain that although it took a bit more thinking, their second sentences are much more specific, informative, and interesting. This is how students should write all year.

When grading student writing, deduct points for weak words. (I let students revise for points back, so they can recoup these points once they replace the weak words with stronger ones.) Students may complain about the extra effort this practice takes, but by the end of the year, they will be keenly aware of their instinct to fall back on these easy words.

Part 2: Crush the Clichés

In another mini-lesson, address clichés. Often, students won't even realize they're using a cliché; we actually think in clichés so often that we hardly notice it. And students usually don't know that clichés make for weak writing. Give small groups paragraphs containing clichés, and have them identify the offending phrases and rewrite them in stronger language. Then hold them responsible for avoiding clichés in their writing throughout the year. Below is an example of a practice paragraph containing ten clichés. (Clichés are noted here; the exercise can be found online without the clichés identified; see Resource 2.)

PRACTICE PARAGRAPH: IDENTIFY AND REWRITE CLICHÉS

I couldn't believe what a fun day I had at the amusement park with my best friend Maria—we're like <u>two peas in a pod</u> at parks. Even though it was <u>raining cats and dogs</u> in the early morning, it was nothing but <u>blue skies</u> for the rest of the day. We went on so many rides that by the afternoon I could have <u>eaten a horse</u>! There was one ride, however, I avoided <u>like the plague</u>: the Whirlwind. You have to stand up inside a giant round tube and get spun around until the friction of the spinning pins you to the wall. I <u>steered clear</u> of that one, but Maria went on it and ended up <u>tossing her cookies</u> after. She <u>got back in the saddle</u> later and went on the Drop of Death with me. <u>Last but not least</u>, we went on the old-fashioned cars. I'm sure I'll <u>sleep like a log</u> tonight!

---

3 Sentence Mash-Up

Sentence combining has long been touted as an effective method to help students work with meaning and practice grammar in context. Several books and websites are dedicated to this practice and provide exercises of varying levels of difficulty. However, I've found that the most effective way to use sentence combining is to create the exercises from the texts we're actually reading in the moment, and to use the exercise as a pre-reading activity. This not only provides content but enhances reading comprehension for the overall text as well. Here are the steps to creating your own sentence-combining exercise.

1. Scan the text for any longer sentences, especially sentences with compound verbs, multiple adjectives, or adverbs. Preferably, find a sentence that is also significant—it touches upon an important aspect of the characterization, setting, plot, or theme, since students will remember the sentence after working with it in this exercise.

2. Find the main subject and verb of the sentence. (This is usually the best place to start but not necessarily the only place; every sentence is different.) Type the subject and verb as a basic sentence.

3. Below, list short, separate sentences for each adjective, adverb, or prepositional phrase. You will repeat the main subject and verb many times. It's also beneficial to use plenty of linking verbs in these sentences—students will see how editing them out can help their writing.

4. Try not to add any larger, more meaningful words—add only linking verbs and mostly use repetition. If your original sentence has a subordinate clause with a word such as *when* or *while*, you could use a phrase such as "at the same time" or "as this was happening." For a clause with *because*, use a phrase like "as a result." Avoid using the conjunctions that are already in the sentence—let students figure out how to combine phrases with the appropriate conjunction.

5. Type directions at the top of your page, and leave space below the sentences for students to work.

At right is an example of a sentence-combining exercise with the famous first sentence from Kafka's (1915) *The Metamorphosis*.

SAMPLE SENTENCE-COMBINING EXERCISE

Directions: Combine the following sentences into one long sentence. You can cut words, add connecting words, and use any necessary punctuation.

Gregor Samsa awoke one morning.

He had had uneasy dreams.

He found himself transformed.

He was transformed in his bed.

He was transformed into a gigantic insect.

(Original: *As Gregor Samsa awoke one morning from uneasy dreams he found himself transformed in his bed into a gigantic insect.*)

This activity works wonderfully in partners and as pre-reading. Students can check their sentences against the author's "answer" and discuss choices the author made in structuring the sentence.

Practice Daily!

I'm a firm believer in the power of small, daily efforts in any area of one's life. With consistent practice, we can improve in anything. This is especially true in the classroom. Short exercises can keep students' minds limber and increase writing fluency. Students could use a small notebook, or separate section of a larger notebook, for these writing calisthenics. In addition to sentence-combining exercises, you could rotate these additional short activities for a brief daily practice. (Note that these practices, taken together, include reflective, narrative, persuasive, and expository elements, as well as sentence structure and editing.)

1. **Journal Jot:** Many books and websites offer ideas for regular journaling; I like to keep journal prompts related to whatever we're reading. For example, when reading *The Outsiders*, I ask, "Ponyboy felt betrayed by Darry. Think of a time when you felt betrayed by someone close to you." I usually set the journal minimum at five sentences. Of course, students could pull any topic from their Life List and let the stream of consciousness flow.

2. **Brainstorm Blast:** Give the class a topic, and have them spend five minutes brainstorming it. The topic could be arguable (like "School Uniforms" or "Homework") or descriptive ("My Yard," "The Cafeteria," "The Beach"). Sensory detail brainstorms are particularly useful and important; training the mind to notice sensory details is not only the key to good writing, but to a life of awareness and appreciation. For extra practice, you could suggest a certain form of brainstorming each week (a list, a web, a Venn diagram, a flow chart, and so on).

3. **Craft a Claim:** Give students a persuasive topic, tell them to choose a side, and have them write a possible claim about it, complete with a reason or two. When they've practiced this a bit, have them write two claims, one for each side of the argument. This simple activity will ingrain the definition and purpose of a claim into students' minds.

4. **Correction Calisthenics:** Take a short paragraph, preferably from a text you are currently reading, and rewrite it with several errors in punctuation, grammar, and spelling. This is especially effective as a pre-reading activity: Use a paragraph from something you will read that day or the next. That way, as students rewrite and correct the paragraph, they will be even more prepared for the upcoming reading. When they return to the text, they will be thinking about grammar and structure as well as content.

4 Model Chop

Through this practice, students will develop a sense of how texts are structured; even though it does not involve writing, it will help students shape their own writing. The idea is simple: Students receive a cold text chopped up into parts; they read the parts and use their understanding of the content as well as their knowledge of organization and transition cues to deduce the original order of the piece.

Short texts, such as essays or short stories, are best. Nonfiction pieces with clear main ideas and examples or stories that progress chronologically will be the easiest for students to work with at first. You could also use a section, such as a chapter, of a longer text. Below are some guidelines.

1. Copy your text; remove anything that would indicate the order of paragraphs, such as page numbers. If there are subtitles, keep them. You might consider copying and pasting the text into a Word document, so that the paragraphs look uniform.

2. Cut the text into strips. These can be several paragraphs per strip, which would be easier, or one paragraph per strip, which would be more challenging. Leave subtitles with the paragraphs that follow them, or, for a more difficult challenge, cut them out singly. Again, try not to give students clues with the physical shape of the strips; the goal here is for students to figure out the order of the piece using content alone. You could even separate paragraphs with two cuts, so that none of the strips fit together on their edges.

3. Shuffle the strips and place them in an envelope. Students can work in pairs to read each strip and discuss how the overall piece should be ordered.

4. When all groups are done, discuss with the whole class what the "answer" is and how the process progressed. What clues helped them arrange the pieces? How did they know the beginning and end? Were there any specific transition words or other cues?

START SMALL

To try an easier version of this exercise, use only a single paragraph. You will definitely have to copy and paste the paragraph into Word so that the sentences are physically uniform. You may or may not want to keep the first sentence indented; the indentation would give away the fact that it is the first sentence, but perhaps that is a visual cue your students should learn. Students will learn to recognize and reassemble the parts of a paragraph.

More Uses With Models

In addition to being fun, imitation writing can be a powerful teaching tool. In order to write imitations or parodies, students must understand the structure and content of the original piece. Then they must work hard to replicate those. Parody writing especially requires higher level skills in understanding content, structure, and literary elements. Here are some tips about how to have your students write imitations and parodies:

1. **Use the material you are already reading.** Have students replicate what they have in front of them—this will cultivate a deep understanding of the original. This works especially well with shorter poems, but if you're reading a longer piece, see if you can extract a paragraph or small section. Perhaps the opening paragraph could work or a featured structure within the text. Even a parody of a single sentence, such as "It was the best of times; it was the worst of times," could be a fun activity which would reinforce an understanding of meaning or structure.

2. **Have students write parodies of songs.** This form of parody has been around for a long time and examples abound. Rewriting songs can help students understand the nature of parody as well as the role of rhyme, meter, repetition, and parallelism. For an added challenge, have students connect the content of their parody to a story read in class.

3. **Have students write mock-umentaries of their readings.** In a mock-umentary format, students reenact scenes, but personal interviews from the characters pepper the action, in which characters comment on plot and the other characters, reveal motivations and traits, make predictions, and create dramatic irony. In creating a mock-umentary, students must fully understand the characters and the characters' inner thoughts. Students can perform or make a video (a better choice for a mock-umentary) of the final product.

4. **Have students write a script or story placing the characters in a different setting.** In groups, students can create a script in which characters retain their traits, backstories, goals, and motivations but find themselves in a new situation. For example, the characters of *Pride and Prejudice* could find themselves stranded on a desert island; the gods from Greek mythology could be thrust into a zombie apocalypse; the gang from *The Outsiders* could wake up in the far future (or the far past). Students should start with stage directions and write a script with a new plot for the characters from their reading.

How to Assign a Parody or Imitation

When assigning a parody or imitation, specify:

- the exact text or part of a text that should be imitated
- the structure of the imitation (poem, paragraph, script)
- the specific aspects of the original that should be preserved (such as rhyme, meter, character traits, structure, introductory technique, tone, and so on)
- the length of the final product (such as a number of lines or pages)
- how the parody should be produced (written/performed/videoed)

NOTE

Because imitation writing can take on any form, I've categorized it as a practice instead of a specific assignment. However, it might be most effective to create an activity sheet like the ones throughout the rest of this book, using your own specifications for imitation writing.

5 Intro Intrigue

Introductions can be tricky. Yet their importance should not be understated: Introductions are the first words a reader encounters about the writer's thoughts. And, unless the reader is a teacher or some other mandatory audience, the reader does not have to continue if she doesn't like what she sees. Get students in the habit of crafting deliberate, interesting, purposeful intros to essays. Here are some suggestions how.

I.   Write the intro last.

This is the most helpful piece of advice I give students about introductions. So many of them would otherwise sit there, staring at a blank page for whole class periods, unable to begin. I tell them to simply rewrite their thesis and get to the body paragraphs. For students who must write something, I tell them to start with a sentence like, "This is my future intro that will change your thoughts about life," or something else silly, so that they can skip to the first body paragraph and get writing. Or, I tell them to purposefully write the worst intro they can about the topic. Or, I urge them to just leave the space blank. I try anything I can just to get students past the intro when they first start to write.

This practice is not just psychological; it's logical: Students can't introduce something until they know what they are introducing. So often, essays or stories reshape themselves in the writing process; reasons change, plots shift, and theses sharpen. It is a loss of energy and time to hammer out intros based on brainstormings.

2.   Start with imagery.

Imagery always works, no matter the genre. After students have written their body paragraphs, one possibility for an intro is to craft a small scene relevant to the thesis that will draw the reader in. As humans, we simply can't resist interesting sensory details. Two or three sentences should suffice. Besides diving right in to a scene, another scaffold for imagery is to begin with "Imagine": "Imagine the clash of armor and ringing of swords as two enemies fight each other to the death. . . ." When students use "Imagine," I often have to caution them with bits of advice. First, they should create a scene a reader could actually imagine. They should also not make the image too simplistic; these sentences should have lots of engaging sensory detail.

3.   Start with a general statement of truth.

Begin with a statement most readers will agree with, and move from the general to the specific. Pronouncements such as "Friendship is built upon trust and laughter" or "Most people want to feel accepted by their community" are ones with which most readers will concur; they will want to keep reading to see where the author is headed. Of course, the writer must then work her way from the general to the specific, taking steps from this broad statement until she reaches her claim.

4. Use a statistic or other interesting fact.

Statistics or other interesting facts have a way of drawing readers in—as with sensory details, our brains are naturally attracted to them and want to know more. A statistic such as "In 2015 . . ." or a fact like "Knights typically wore 40 pounds of armor as they entered into battle" piques curiosity.

5. Use a creative definition or famous quotation.

Many teachers think using a dictionary definition to begin a piece is clichéd, and it can be—but writers still do it when appropriate. If the word is truly unusual and engaging, or foreign, or defined in an uncommon way, it could work. The same is true for famous quotations: they can be engaging if used effectively. Students must understand the quotation fully before they use it, and then they must move convincingly from the quotation to their claim. I advise students to use both of these methods sparingly, but I don't discourage them from trying; as new writers, they must become familiar with all the tricks of the trade, even the time-worn ones.

6 Cultivate a Conclusion

Most students affirm that writing strong conclusions is more difficult than writing effective introductions. They know what a conclusion is, but they are not exactly sure how to write one beyond simply repeating the main points of what they've said. Somehow, though, a conclusion should take the paper's ideas one step further. That "somehow" will be different for every piece. As writers, students must look at the entire piece of writing and decide what ending would be best.

I tell students plainly that conclusions take thought, effort and time—they shouldn't panic if one doesn't come right away. Here is a list of some options:

CONCLUSION TECHNIQUES

1. Summarize the main points *in different words*. (I review what "summarize" means and stress that this option should be combined with another of those listed below.)

2. Give an opinion.

3. Give a brief anecdote that illustrates the main points of the essay, or create a scenario that does the same.

4. Personalize the topic by explaining what it has taught you about life or how your life has changed/is better because of it.

5. Give a solution to the problem or create a call to action. A strong clincher with this method could use an "if/then" sentence.

6. Give a general statement of truth, such as "One must follow his or her conscience" or "People will find time for what is important to them," and explain how it relates.

7. Relate the topic or theme to the modern day, explaining what it would look and feel like now.

8. Pick up where you left off in the Introduction, thereby creating a frame for the entire piece.

Different assignments will require different conclusions. For example, a process essay could end well with number 4, a personalization of the topic. Number 3, an anecdote, could neatly finish a compare and contrast essay, as could number 2. Number 5, a solution or call to action, is a classic technique for concluding a persuasive essay, and number 6, a general statement of truth, may be appropriate for the personal essay. But these recommendations are not orders; encourage the students to try anything that seems interesting and to try it with confidence. Somehow, though, they must do something new at the end of their writing; they cannot simply repeat what they have already said. This extra thought is often what will take the entire piece to a new level.

CLINCHERS: "DROP THE MIC"

The very last sentence of a piece can be difficult to craft. Jen Tarr, a colleague of mine, tells students they should feel like they could "drop the mic" after their last sentence.

7 Amp Up the Verbs!

Verbs pump the blood of a sentence. As writers, students must try to use the most specific verbs possible. The good news is that most students already know enough strong verbs, if they look closely and think. Put these sentences on the screen or board:

> *As I went down the hall, I saw him from the corner of my eye. I knew he was the one who stood up to a bully for me. I was nervous. Should I go up to him? I decided I would, and I turned quickly and went toward him.*

Have students copy the paragraph in their notebooks and underline all the verbs. (It may be necessary to review the definition of "verb.") Ask them to think of any better replacements for the underlined verbs and to write them in. Most students will recognize the first verb, *went*, as rather dry and will replace it with *walked*. This is better, but ask if there are any other verbs that are even more descriptive than *walked*? Suggest visualizing the person walking. How is he/she walking? Generate a short list of "Words Instead of *Walk*" beside the paragraph. It might include terms like *strolled, sauntered, skipped, rushed, strode,* and *strutted*. Suggest that to "see someone from the corner of your eye" is a bit of a cliché; is there a verb or verb phrase that could replace the whole phrase? Verbs like *glimpsed, spied,* and *spotted* might suffice.

How about *stand up*? Advise the students to always question two-part verbs, that is, verbs that have a preposition attached to them. Sometimes they can't be avoided, but many times they are replaceable. In this case, a verb such as *defended* or *protected* would work, though the sentence would have to be slightly rearranged to accommodate it; this is okay. Some students will then spot *go up* as a two-part verb, and replace it with *approach, greet, face,* or *thank*. Tell students to also watch for weak verbs paired with an adverb, like *turn quickly*. Could they eliminate the adverb with a more precise verb? Perhaps *spun* or *whirled* might be better.

Tell the class about the archenemy of strong verbs: an overuse of the word *is* in all its forms (*am, are, was, were*). Of course, *is* by itself is a linking verb that has no action. If writers use too many sentences without action, the piece starts to feel dry and boring. Advise that they try to use only one linking verb per paragraph. Ask students: *Do you see any in this paragraph?* You can let the first stay, but push the class on the second one. Students will immediately offer the word *felt*, which is slightly better sounding than *was*, but technically still a linking verb. Suggest that they take

ACTIVITY: WHY ACTION VERBS ROCK

1. Write different verbs, both active and linking, each on their own index cards and invite students to perform the action on the card they are given.

2. The students who receive cards with action verbs must dance, sing, twirl, hop, and so on, to the delight of the class.

3. The students who receive cards with linking verbs just shrug and stand there, to the disappointment of the class.

4. Explain: That's what it feels like in writing as well.

the most important part of the sentence and attach it to another sentence either before or after. Students should recognize that *nervous* should be salvaged; ask them if they could attach it to another sentence. The revised paragraph might sound like this:

> *As I rushed down the hall, I glimpsed him to my right. I knew he was the one who defended me to a bully. Nervous, I wondered if I should approach him. I decided I would, spun on my heel, and strode toward him.*

Notice that most students would already know the above verbs. As a practice, have students find five weak verbs in their writings, replace them, and show the revisions on their rough drafts.

Post It!

Have class discussions to generate lists of Words Instead of *Said,* Words Instead of *Walk,* Words Instead of *Laugh,* and so on. Post these as signs in the classroom or on the class website so students can refer to them at any time.

WAYS TO STRENGTHEN VERBS

1. Visualize the action clearly and try to think of a more specific word.

2. Try to replace two-part verbs (verbs that have a preposition attached to them).

3. Try to replace verbs that need an adverb. Is there one word that could say both?

4. Try to limit *is, am, was, were* to one per paragraph. You may need to rearrange sentences.

8 · Editing Check Sheets

Having students revise and edit on their own helps them grow into self-sufficient writers and thinkers. These four editing/revising check sheets, available online (see page 127), can get students thinking like writers. You could start the year with the first check sheet, and graduate students to the second after a quarter or semester. Use the Narrative and Analysis check sheets as needed.

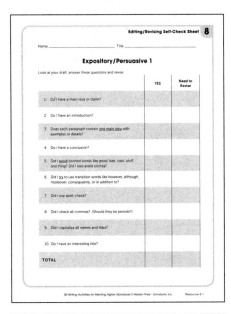

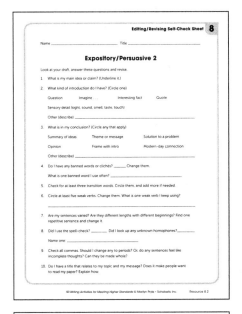

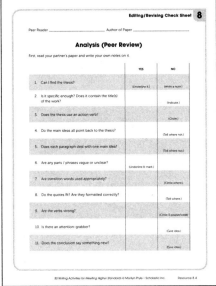

Resources 8.1–8.4, Editing Check Sheets, are available online; see page 127 for instructions on how to access.

Narrative Writing

Narrative is the heart of all human history, culture, and identity. In addition, strong narrative writing focuses on sensory details, a staple of effective writing in any genre. The writing assignments in this section are comprised of autobiography, fiction, and poetry. The standards at right are addressed in each activity.

As will appear in each block of Individual Writing Activities, below are some specific thoughts for each assignment. You'll find the corresponding Writing Assignments and Prewriting Sheets on pages 27–55. Writing models are available online; see page 127 for instructions on how to access.

9 Setting Sketch

The Setting Sketch is one of my favorite writing activities for several reasons. First, it is autobiographical, about a place the student knows well, a place that holds some meaning in his or her life. The student is the expert here, a juxtaposition I like to introduce at the beginning of the year. Second, its main focus is on the generation of sensory detail, which is the foundation of strong writing in any genre. And third, the Setting Sketch provides an opportunity to discuss a rudimentary idea of theme, the answer to the reader's question, "Why should I care?" These three elements—using one's life, seeing sensory details, and giving a reason to care—are the cornerstones of communication. After writing a Setting Sketch, one can go anywhere. The model writing is available online as Resource 9.3; see page 127 for instructions on how to access.

MAIN STANDARD
Write narratives to express actual or fictionalized experiences or events using purposeful strategies, effective details, and clear organizational techniques.

ADDITIONAL STANDARDS
▸ Generate cohesive pieces focusing on the assignment, purpose, and audience.

▸ Participate in the writing process (reading, prewriting, drafting, revising, and editing).

▸ Demonstrate a clear understanding of the conventions of English.

▸ Demonstrate an ability to use effective figurative language and appropriate vocabulary depending on assignment, purpose, and audience.

10 Character Sketch

Like the Setting Sketch, the Character Sketch asks students to use their lives, or specifically, the people in them, as fertile ground for ideas. Usually, these pieces are the most moving ones I get all year. How often do we really look closely at the people we love? You'll notice that instead of a Prewriting Sheet, I give a list of questions: In my experience, a live, whole-class, teacher-led brainstorming works well for this assignment. Of course, if this is not possible, simply copy or post the questions for students. Also similar to the Setting Sketch, the Character Sketch continues the use of sensory details and a basic notion of theme. Remember, though, that both of these assignments are just sketches, not full stories with a developed plot and climax. The focus is on description. Notice too that the elements of characterization (what a character looks like, does, and says) are highlighted here; after completing this activity, students will more readily recognize characterization techniques in their reading as well. The model writing is available online as Resource 10.3; see page 127 for instructions on how to access.

11 Free Verse Memory Poem

This assignment stays with the practice of using sensory detail, but expands from only description to a short plot, in the form of a memory. The Prewriting Sheet harkens back to the Setting and Character Sketches. Other forms of figurative language are emphasized here as well. The model writing is available online as Resource 11.3; see page 127 for instructions on how to access.

12 Autobiographical Incident

Now that students have a grasp of setting and character (if they did the previous activities), they are ready to write out fuller plots. Note that this activity includes Prewriting Sheet: Short Story, which is referred to in several upcoming activities. The element of theme is deepened here to include the concept of what the main character learned. Since the piece is autobiographical, students must ask themselves what they learned in the incident—this may be difficult to frame at first. During conferences, reassure students that the "lesson" might be something as simple as realizing how much they love their family, or learning one should always be grateful for time with friends. Above all, stress to students that any event, viewed honestly and closely, can have meaning. This is the assignment that prompts many students to claim that they "have nothing to write" or that "nothing interesting happens" in their lives. Assure them that if they are alive, they have stories to tell. The model writing is available online as Resource 12.5; see page 127 for instructions on how to access. NOTE: The Prewriting Sheet: Short Story is also used in #13, Proverb Story; #14, Retelling of a Legend; #18, Living Legend; #19, Short Story; and #20, Historical Fiction.

> **BONUS STANDARD**
> Since this assignment includes a partner questionnaire, the skills of effective listening and speaking are included. This questionnaire can be used with any subsequent story-based activity.

13 Proverb Story

This is another version of the autobiographical account, but students are required to do a bit of research as well. If any of your in-class readings reference a culture's aphorisms, this assignment would make a fun complementary activity. A twist here is that the chosen proverb *is* the theme at the end. Encourage students to incorporate it creatively—maybe one of the characters says the proverb or the main character finds it scrawled on her notebook cover—even if it didn't happen that way in the real story. A little writer's license can be acceptable here! The model writing is available online as Resource 13.3; see page 127 for instructions on how to access.

14 Retelling of a Legend

After students have written autobiographical accounts, this activity can help them branch into fiction. However, they don't yet have to think of a story from scratch—they can retell a story from family or cultural legend. The elements of having a developed setting, character, plot, and theme still apply. The model writing is available online as Resource 14.3; see page 127 for instructions on how to access.

15 Historical Ballad

This assignment may involve a bit of research in order to craft a meaningful poem about an actual person or event in history. For model reading, use Alfred Noyes's "The Highwayman" (about a historical time) or the anonymously written "John Henry" (about an actual person). Stress to students that their ballads don't have to completely rhyme or even rhyme at all, as this can be a major obstacle to meaning and flow for fledgling writers. Students should, if possible, incorporate a refrain, which is often a staple of the traditional ballad. The model writing is "The Highwayman," which is available online as Resource 15.3; see page 127 for instructions on how to access.

16 Personal Ballad

This activity is modeled after Li Po's famous "The River-Merchant's Wife: A Letter," translated by Ezra Pound. Unlike the historical ballads referenced in #15, Li Po's ballad is much more intimate and more informal—it does not rhyme or have a refrain. The stanzas are arranged by age, and the mood and meaning is communicated through imagery. Students will use memories and images from their own lives to create their own personal ballads. Remind students that the memories do not have to be "life or death"—quiet memories of small moments lodged in their minds work beautifully too. The model writing is available online as Resource 16.3; see page 127 for instructions on how to access.

17 Children's Book

Here, students can try completely inventing a story on their own, focusing on figurative language along with a basic sense of characters, setting, and plot. The best model reading here would be actual children's books. Bring in boxes of them and let students browse through as many as they can. The Prewriting Sheet for this activity focuses heavily on the elements of plot and the importance of point of view, both of which could make useful mini-lessons if needed.

BONUS STANDARD
Since Activities #14, #15, and #20 involve research, the skills of finding and evaluating various sources, paraphrasing, and citing are incorporated.

PARTNER UP
Given the difficulty involved in the research and poetic elements for the Historical Ballad, it might be best completed in partners. Finished products could be illustrated or posted to the class site.

SHARE IT
When Children's Books are completed, have students read them aloud to younger classes.

You could have students create the finished products of the books on paper or online. The Storyboard: Children's Book sheet students use to plan their books is available online as Resource 17.3; see page 127 for instructions on how to access.

18 Living Legend

This activity requires students to interview an older person, find a singular "moment" that would make an interesting short story, and retell that story in the first person. I usually have students come up with a bunch of possible interview questions so they don't go into the interview blank. I tell them that if, in the middle of asking the questions, they find a "moment" that could be the story, they can abandon the remaining questions and focus only on that moment. Students should get as much information from their interviewees as possible, but they may have to do additional research about the era in order to fill in details about the setting or dress. And because this is a short story, there should be a theme—this usually makes for a meaningful conclusion. Encourage students to ask the interviewee what he or she learned or realized from the event. I usually set the interviewee age at 50 or above (this seems ancient to them!), but I encourage them to think of the oldest person they feel comfortable talking to. Common topics include: how grandparents met, when a child (usually the student's mother or father) was born, anything involving a war event, immigration into the country, and funny moments from childhood. These pieces make an engaging and moving anthology, especially at the end of the year. The model writing is available online as Resource 18.3; see page 127 for instructions on how to access.

19 Short Story

The official "Short Story" is included at the end of this block (as opposed to the beginning) because ideally students should have experience with developing setting, character, plot, theme, and point of view if they are to write meaningful, interesting short fiction. For model reading, use a short story from your curriculum, or find something new—I like to use Shirley Jackson's "Charles" or Kate Chopin's "Story of an Hour," both for their brevity and surprise endings. It's possible that students won't use all the information they're asked to brainstorm, but that's okay: It's always better for a writer to know more about his stories than needed. The model writing is available online as Resource 19.4; see page 127 for instructions on how to access.

> **PREWRITING SHEET: SHORT STORY**
>
> **Prewriting Sheet: Short Story** is used in writing activities #12, #13, #14, #18, #19, and #20. It appears on pages 37–38 and online in the Resource Pages of each activity that calls for it.

20 Historical Fiction

A mini-lesson about the elements of historical fiction would surely help students here. Use their prior knowledge of books and movies to create a list of guidelines for historical fiction. For sample reading, use a chapter from current class text if possible, or photocopy a chapter from another book. (I like to use the first chapter from *The Devil's Arithmetic*.) Students should cite their research, and when writing, incorporate what they know about crafting effective fiction—just because something is historical doesn't mean one can overlook character, setting, plot, theme, and point of view! These pieces often turn out to be longer, more in-depth products; be prepared to allot more time, perhaps a week or two, for students to work. The two Prewriting Sheets are available online as Resources 20.3 and 20.4; see page 127 for instructions on how to access.

Name _____ Date _____

Setting Sketch

☐ 1. Read the sample setting sketch, and answer the questions at the bottom of that paper.

☐ 2. Think of an interesting place. It can be a favorite place, or a place that is memorable in some way. It should be somewhere that you have been to in person. Be careful not to choose too large of an area (e.g., New York City is too big to describe, but a street in Brooklyn is okay).

☐ 3. Complete the **Prewriting Sheet: Setting Sketch**.

☐ 4. Be sure to explain why the place is important to you (#9). This will be the conclusion (ending).

☐ 5. Write a first draft describing this place. You can put yourself in the scene, but don't give it any action. Remember, this is just a description and not a whole story.

☐ 6. Write enough for at least _____ page(s).

☐ 7. Make sure you use one of your details right in the first sentence. This will be an interesting introduction.

☐ 8. Revise what you have written. Upgrade three verbs. Give the piece a title. Edit your work.

☐ 9. Submit your prewriting, drafts, final copy, and this sheet.

		Preliminary Grade	Revised Grade
Structure (paragraphs, length, title)	20%		
Process (questions, prewriting, drafts)	20%		
Ideas (sensory details, theme)	20%		
Language (no banned words, clichés, wordiness)	20%		
Grammar/Spelling (punctuation, tenses, sentences, _____)	20%		
TOTAL			

Name _____ Date _____

Setting Sketch

1. Place:

2. Sights and Colors	
3. Sounds	4. Textures and Temperature
5. Smells	6. Tastes (if any)

7. Is there any special history to this place? What was it before you were there?

8. Think of an interesting detail to begin with in your first sentence. Look at your ideas above. Which one will you start with?

9. Why is this place important to you? What does it mean to you? (This will be your ending.)

10. Remember that a sketch is only a description, not a full story. Nothing needs to happen here, although you can put yourself in the scene in order to describe it.

Name _____ Date _____

Character Sketch

1. Read the sample character sketch, and answer the questions that follow.

2. On paper, answer the **Prewriting Questions: Character Sketch**.

3. Now, write out your sketch, using your answers to the Prewriting Questions—the description, the verbs, the words. Weave it all together. Use the present tense. Remember that this is only a description and not a whole story.

4. At the end of your description, write a paragraph about the importance of the person to you. The entire piece should be at least _____ page(s).

5. Revise your draft and upgrade three verbs. Give the piece a title. Edit your work.

6. Submit your prewriting, drafts, final copy, and this sheet.

		Preliminary Grade	Revised Grade
Structure (paragraphs, length, title)	20%		
Process (questions, prewriting, drafts)	20%		
Ideas (sensory details, actions, sayings, theme)	20%		
Language (no banned words, clichés, wordiness)	20%		
Grammar/Spelling (punctuation, tenses, sentences, _____)	20%		
TOTAL			

Character Sketch

Note: For this assignment, I read aloud the following questions and students answer in writing.

1. Choose a person that you know well—family members or close friends. No pets.

2. Below the person's name, write "Looks."

3. Close your eyes for a moment and picture that person. As ideas come into your mind, write them down in a big list under the word "Looks." How does the person look? Write down anything you can about his or her physical appearance. You can use just one-word phrases or longer phrases, but don't write whole sentences. This is just a list of ideas. *I usually give a few minutes here, and then continue.*

   • Is the person tall or short, or in the middle?

   • Is he or she thin, medium, or stout? Muscular? Small?

   • Is the person young, middle-aged, or old? How can you tell?

   • What is the eye color? The hair color? What is the hair style?

   • Look closely at the person's face. What do you see?

   • Is there anything interesting about the eyes, the eyebrows? Does the person have a mustache or beard?

   • What is the smile like? Big? Shy? Crooked?

   • What does the person usually wear? If pants, what kind? What style shirt? Describe the shoes.

   • Look at the person's hands. Is there anything notable about them?

   • Is he or she dark-skinned, light-skinned, olive, pale, or freckled?

   • Does the person usually wear a certain piece of jewelry, like a necklace, bracelet, or ring? Describe it.

   • Does the person usually carry something, like a wallet or purse, a phone, or some kind of good luck charm or religious item?

   • What are some of the person's favorite belongings?

   • How does the person smell? Does he or she commonly smell like coffee, for example, or a certain perfume? (*I realize I'm sneaking this one in under "Looks," but a person's smell contributes, I think, to the overall physical impact.*)

4. Leave some space under this list in case anything else comes to mind. If it does, just jot it down, even if you're in the middle of another section. Find a new space, either to the side or on the back of the paper, and write down "Actions." This will be a section for what the person *does*. I want you to use verb phrases here.

continued on next page

   50 Writing Activities for Meeting Higher Standards © Marilyn Pryle • Scholastic Inc.

- Think of the person again. Is there something, some habit, that he or she is always doing? For example, does he *tap* his foot or fingers? (*I usually write these phrases on the board after I demonstrate them, starting with the verb.*) Does she *twirl* her hair? Does he constantly *stare* at his phone? Does she *yawn* all the time because she never gets enough sleep? Does she *overstuff* her purse so she can't find anything? Does he always *misplace* his glasses? Does she often *clear* her throat when talking?

- What does the person do that makes him who he is today? Does the person have any rituals or routines that happen regularly, over time? How about the person's career? Try to think of these in the present perfect or present perfect progressive tense. For example, has he flown planes for 20 years? Has she cooked dinner every day for ten years? You would say, he *has flown* planes or she *has cooked* dinner . . . Another example: He *has been reading* the newspaper every morning since he turned 15.

- Think of how the person walks. Try to think of another verb besides *walk* to describe what it looks like. Does the person *shuffle* or *drag* his feet? Does she often *stumble* or *trip*? Does he *swagger* or *saunter*? Does she *tiptoe* or *skip*? Does he or she *stomp*? Does anyone want to demonstrate a walk so we can find a verb for it?

- Think of the person's laugh. Try to describe it with a precise verb. Does the person *giggle, hiccup,* or *chirp*? Does he *guffaw*? Does she *snort*? Does he *choke*? Any demonstrations?

- Think of how the person speaks. Try to find a word to describe it. Does she *squeak*? Does he *growl*? Does the person often *whisper* or *yell*? Any demonstrations?

5. Leave some space after that section and find another spot on your paper. Go to a new page if you have to. Next I want you to think of what the person commonly *says*. What are some phrases you might hear the person say?

   - Does the person have a certain greeting, like "What's up, dude?"

   - Does the person have a nickname for you?

   - Does the person always want to do something? For example, you know that when you see the person, he or she will most likely say, "Let's go to the mall!" or "Let's watch the game!" or "Want to play video games?" or "How about a game of cards?"

   - Does the person often complain about something? For example, does he or she often say, "I wish we didn't have homework!" or "I hate the winter!"

6. Now, go to another space on your paper and think about why this person is important to you. What have you learned from this person? Write a few sentences that come to mind.

7. Finally, think of a place that you can imagine your person in. What does he or she like to do? Where do you usually see him or her? What is he or she doing? It doesn't have to be something unusual or special; it should be an everyday place where you commonly see the person.

continued on next page

- Once you have a scene in your mind, think about your five senses.

- What are the sights in this scene? What objects are around? What colors?

- What is the light like? If it is outside, is it sunny, cloudy, dim, or nighttime?

- What are the sounds?

- What are some smells?

- What are some physical feelings? Is it cold or hot? What are some textures?

Remember, this is not a story; it is only a description. Nothing big should happen in this scene. The person is just doing some small thing he or she always does.

50 Writing Activities for Meeting Higher Standards © Marilyn Pryle • Scholastic Inc

Name _____   Date _____

Free Verse Memory Poem

☐   1.   A free verse poem does not have a set rhyme pattern or meter. You will write one about a memory in your life.

☐   2.   Read the sample poems. Notice the colors, sights, sounds, textures, and smells. Answer the questions given.

☐   3.   Complete the **Prewriting Sheet: Free Verse Memory Poem**.

☐   4.   Write a first draft of your poem using the ideas from your Prewriting Sheet. You can use short lines or long lines. Remember that a poem is not a paragraph—it is broken up into lines.

☐   5.   An interesting way to end the poem could be with what you learned (#4 on the Prewriting Sheet). You could also try to use an image (a sensory detail) in the last line.

☐   6.   Revise your draft. Add **three more sensory details** and give it a title. Your poem should be at least _____ lines long.

☐   7.   Submit your prewriting, drafts, final copy, and this sheet.

- -

		Preliminary Grade	Revised Grade
Structure (poem format, length, title)	20%		
Process (questions, prewriting, drafts)	20%		
Ideas (details, implied theme)	20%		
Language (no banned words, clichés, wordiness)	20%		
Grammar/Spelling (punctuation, capitals, tenses, _____)	20%		
TOTAL			

Name _____ Date _____

Free Verse Memory Poem

1. **Plot:** What is your memory? Summarize it on the back. (Be careful to choose a single moment in time, not a week-long event.)

2. **Setting:** Think of some sensory details about where your memory took place:

    Sights and Colors: Sounds:

    Textures and Touch: Smells:

3. Were you or other people in this story? List them in a chart like this on the back, and give details for each:

Person	Details (clothes, height, hair, eyes, verbs, etc.)

4. **Theme:** How did this memory end? What did you learn or realize? Write about it on the back.

5. **Figurative Language:** Look at all of your details on your chart.

Add a simile (like/as) to your setting.	Change a sound to onomatopoeia.	Add another color to a sight.
Add some personification.	Pick a detail and try to use alliteration with it.	Choose a sight, and add a texture about it.

    50 Writing Activities for Meeting Higher Standards © Marilyn Pryle • Scholastic Inc.

Name _____ Date _____

Autobiographical Incident

- [ ] 1. Read the sample incident and answer the questions given.

- [ ] 2. Think of some times in your life that you remember well. Think of some moments when you felt happy, sad, scared, excited, nervous, or proud. They can be recent or from long ago. Pick one of these memories to write about.

- [ ] 3. Complete the **Prewriting Sheet: Autobiographical Incident** and the **Prewriting Sheet: Short Story**, and complete the **Partner Interview: Autobiographical Incident**.

- [ ] 4. Write a first draft of your story. Read it and add five more sensory details. Your story should be at least _____ page(s).

- [ ] 5. Make sure your story ends with a theme. Explain what you learned from this event.

- [ ] 6. Revise what you have written. Upgrade three verbs. Give the piece a title, and edit your work.

- [ ] 7. Submit your prewriting, drafts, final copy, and this sheet.

		Preliminary Grade	Revised Grade
Structure (paragraphs, length, title)	20%		
Process (questions, prewriting, drafts)	20%		
Ideas (setting, characters, details, theme)	20%		
Language (no banned words, clichés, wordiness)	20%		
Grammar/Spelling (punctuation, tenses, sentences, _____)	20%		
TOTAL			

Name _____ Date _____

Autobiographical Incident

Choose a real event that happened in your life. It can be positive or negative. Make sure the event is brief—don't write about a one-week vacation or entire sports season. Choose a moment. Use these questions to help you; write your answers on a separate sheet of paper.

Memory Generators

1. Think about your life. Write down any strong memory that comes to mind now.

2. Write down any time that was happy.

3. Write down any time that was peaceful and calm.

4. Write down a time you felt proud. Maybe you had done something difficult; maybe you had worked a long time for something; maybe you made the right choice about something.

5. Write down a time you were scared.

6. Write down a time that was very funny; you couldn't stop laughing. What happened?

7. Write down a time when you learned something about life.

8. Write down a time with your family that stands out in your mind.

9. Write down a time with your friends that stands out.

10. Write down a memory from when you were a small child that you still remember today.

Now, choose one memory from your brainstorm and write out a paragraph about it.

50 Writing Activities for Meeting Higher Standards © Marilyn Pryle • Scholastic Inc.

Name _____ Date _____

Short Story

1. **Characters:** Pick the two main people in your story. You can brainstorm more people on a separate sheet. Name them here:

    1. _____   2. _____

    What does your main character care about most? What does he or she want?

    What does he/she fear?

    Now describe your characters in detail:

Person #1:	
Build and clothes (in this story only):	Face, hair, eyes, smells:
Actions or habits (use verbs):	Hobbies? Favorite possessions?
Sayings or dialect:	Family:

continued on next page

Person #2:	
Build and clothes (in this story only):	Face, hair, eyes, smells:
Actions or habits (use verbs):	Hobbies? Favorite possessions?
Sayings or dialect:	Family:

2. **Theme:** What did you (or the main character) learn from this incident? What did you realize about life, or yourself? (This can be your conclusion to the story.)

3. **Setting:** Where did your story happen? _____

   • Describe the sights and colors:

   • Describe the light and weather:

   • Describe the sounds. Use at least **two words** of onomatopoeia:

   • Describe the smells:

   • Describe any textures or temperatures:

   • Look above at what you have written so far. Add two similes somewhere.

4. **Intro:** Start with one of your sensory details from the setting. Which one would make an interesting first sentence? Also, what could be an interesting or clever title?

50 Writing Activities for Meeting Higher Standards © Marilyn Pryle • Scholastic Inc.

Name _____ Date _____

Autobiographical Incident

Partner 1: Explain your topic to your partner. Tell what happened. Then let your partner ask you questions. While he/she does, you can add more notes to your prewriting paper.

Partner 2: Ask any questions that you want to know about the story. Here are some to think about, but you do not have to ask all of them—choose the questions that you like.

1.   How big was this place?

2.   Was it sunny, cloudy, raining, or something else? (for outdoor stories)

3.   Was it daytime or nighttime? Was it bright out or dim?

4.   What other things were in the room? (for indoor stories)

5.   What colors do you remember?

6.   Was it hot or cold there?

7.   What were you wearing?

8.   How old were you?

9.   What was the season? What did it look like outside?

10.   Did you smell anything?

11.   Describe the other person's eyes and hair.

12.   What was the other person wearing? What were the other people wearing?

13.   What were some other sounds or noises?

14.   What was happening in the background?

15.   What did you learn from this?

Name _____   Date _____

Proverb Story

☐ 1. Read the sample story and answer the questions given.

☐ 2. A **proverb** (or **aphorism**) is a wise saying that embodies a truth about life. All cultures have their own proverbs, such as "The wise person has long ears and a short tongue" (German) or "Be not afraid of going slowly; be only afraid of standing still" (Chinese). Research several proverbs, and fill out the top part of the **Prewriting Sheet: Proverb Story**.

☐ 3. You will write your own autobiographical story and end it with the proverb as your theme. You can weave the proverb in to the end of your story in any creative way that you like. Complete the **Prewriting Sheet: Proverb Story** and the **Prewriting Sheet: Short Story**.

☐ 4. Write a first draft of your story. Read it and add more details. Your story should be at least _____ page(s).

☐ 5. Make sure your story ends with your chosen proverb as your theme. Give the piece a title.

☐ 6. Revise and edit. Upgrade three verbs.

☐ 7. Submit your prewriting, drafts, final copy, and this sheet.

		Preliminary Grade	Revised Grade
Structure (paragraphs, length, title)	20%		
Process (questions, prewriting, drafts)	20%		
Ideas (setting, characters, details, theme/proverb)	20%		
Language (no banned words, clichés, wordiness)	20%		
Grammar/Spelling (punctuation, tenses, sentences, _____)	20%		
TOTAL			

Name _____ Date _____

Proverb Story

Research at least five proverbs from various cultures which you find interesting. Write the proverbs below, the cultures they came from, and an explanation of each proverb's meaning.

	Proverb	Culture	Meaning
1.			
2.			
3.			
4.			
5.			

Can any of these proverbs relate to a time in your life? Star one, and write a paragraph below about how it pertains to a true event that you have experienced. If none of the proverbs apply, research more proverbs until you find one that works.

Name _____   Date _____

Retelling of a Legend

☐ 1. Read the sample legend and answer the questions given.

☐ 2. Think of a story about a person or hero that someone told you about, or that you read about somewhere. It could be about a person who lived long ago, or someone more recent. It could be a family legend about someone in your own family.

☐ 3. Complete the **Prewriting Sheet: Retelling of a Legend** and the **Prewriting Sheet: Short Story**.

☐ 4. Write a first draft of your story. Remember that legends are usually told in third person point of view. Read it and add more exaggeration and details (sights, sounds, smells, textures and tastes).

☐ 5. Make sure your story has a theme. Tell what the main character learned from this event. Your story should be at least _____ page(s).

☐ 6. Revise and edit your draft. Upgrade three verbs. Give the piece a title.

☐ 7. Submit your prewriting, drafts, final copy, and this sheet.

		Preliminary Grade	Revised Grade
Structure (paragraphs, length, title)	20%		
Process (questions, prewriting, drafts)	20%		
Ideas (setting, characters, details, exaggeration, theme)	20%		
Language (no banned words, clichés, wordiness)	20%		
Grammar/Spelling (punctuation, tenses, sentences, _____)	20%		
TOTAL			

    50 Writing Activities for Meeting Higher Standards © Marilyn Pryle • Scholastic Inc.

Name _____ Date _____

Retelling of a Legend

What will your legend be about? **Summarize** what happens in your legend, and research details if necessary. List your sources on the back. Use these questions as your guide:

1. Who is the main character?

2. Legends are often about main characters with a special talent or quality. What special talents or qualities does your main character have? You can exaggerate or embellish!

3. Where does the story happen?

4. What is the problem or conflict for this character?

5. What does he/she want?

6. What does the character do to fix the problem or get what he/she wants?

7. Where does the character go at the end?

Legends often have **exaggeration** or **hyperbole** in them. Look back at #2 above, and add some more exaggeration. You can use similes, such as, "She was as strong as a bear" or "He was as gentle as a cloud."

Add exaggeration to #4, the conflict. Make it sound bigger than it was.

As you complete the **Prewriting Sheet: Short Story**, be sure to exaggerate in at least three places. Label your exaggeration.

Name _____ Date _____

Historical Ballad

☐ 1. A **ballad** is a poem that tells a story, often about a hero. Traditionally, ballads have a refrain (a line or lines that are repeated) and may have a rhyme scheme. Read the sample ballad and answer the following:

- Who is this ballad about? How is the person described?

- What is the conflict in the ballad?

- How is the conflict resolved?

- Does this ballad have a refrain or rhyme scheme? What is it?

- List five sensory details from the ballad.

☐ 2. Think of a historical event or person you could write a ballad about. Research the event or person, and complete the **Prewriting Sheet: Historical Ballad**. Cite your source(s) on the back.

☐ 3. Write a first draft of your ballad, using the ideas from your Prewriting Sheet. You can use short lines or long lines. Remember that a poem is not a paragraph—it is broken up into lines. Be sure to have a refrain in your ballad.

☐ 4. Revise your first draft. Add **three more sensory details** and type up a final draft. Your poem should be at least _____ lines long. Give your poem a title.

☐ 5. Submit your prewriting, drafts, final copy, and this sheet.

		Preliminary Grade	Revised Grade
Structure (poem format, length, title)	20%		
Process (questions, prewriting, drafts)	20%		
Ideas (setting, characters, details, theme, refrain)	20%		
Language (no banned words, clichés, wordiness)	20%		
Grammar/Spelling (punctuation, tenses, sentences, _____)	20%		
TOTAL			

50 Writing Activities for Meeting Higher Standards © Marilyn Pryle • Scholastic Inc.

Name _____   Date _____

Historical Ballad

1. **Plot: Who or what** will your ballad be about?

    What is the **conflict** in your ballad? Describe it fully.

    How is the conflict **resolved**?

2. **Setting:** What is the time and place of this story?

    Think of (or research) some details for it:

Sights and Colors:	Sounds:
Textures and Touch:	Smells:

3. **Characterization:** Give some details for the main person/people in your story:

Person	Details (clothes, height, hair, eyes, verbs, etc.)

4. **Figurative Language:** Look at all of your details above, and do the following.

    ☐ Add a simile (*like/as*) to your setting.

    ☐ Change a sound to onomatopoeia.

    ☐ Add another color to a sight.

5. **Refrain:** Think about your story. What line(s) could you write that could be a refrain?

Name _____ Date _____

Personal Ballad

☐ 1. A **ballad** is a poem that tells a story about a person or event. You will write a ballad about yourself using some milestones or memories from your life. Read the sample personal ballad. Notice how each stanza represents a different age of the speaker. Also, notice how the images show how the speaker is feeling.

☐ 2. On the **Brainstorming Chart: Personal Ballad**, brainstorm at least **four milestones or memories** in your life. They can be big or small.

☐ 3. Next to each memory, brainstorm several **images** (sight, sound, smell, taste, touch) that you remember from that moment. Choose images that show how you were feeling in the memory.

☐ 4. Write a rough draft of your poem. In your first line, use an image to show how old you were.

☐ 5. Make each memory its own stanza. Use your brainstormed details to pack each stanza with images as you retell the memory. Have at least **five lines in each stanza**.

☐ 6. Think of a meaningful ending that could tie your memories together. Now add a title.

☐ 7. Revise your poem and upgrade three verbs. Edit your work.

☐ 8. Submit your prewriting, drafts, final copy, and this sheet.

		Preliminary Grade	Revised Grade
Structure (poem format, length, title)	20%		
Process (questions, prewriting, drafts)	20%		
Ideas (4 memories, images/details, theme)	20%		
Language (no banned words, clichés, wordiness)	20%		
Grammar/Spelling (punctuation, tenses, sentences, _____)	20%		
TOTAL			

50 Writing Activities for Meeting Higher Standards © Marilyn Pryle • Scholastic Inc.

Name _____ Date _____

Personal Ballad

List memories	Sights	Sounds	Smells	Taste	Touch
Memory #1					
Memory #2					
Memory #3					
Memory #4					

Name _____ Date _____

Children's Book

☐ 1. Take three of the children's books in the classroom, read them, and answer the following for each:

  • Who is in this book?

  • What does this character want?

  • How does the character get what he/she wants?

  • Find at least two examples of sensory details, similes, or personification.

☐ 2. You will write your own children's book. Fill out the **Prewriting Sheet: Children's Book**.

☐ 3. Write a rough draft of your story.

☐ 4. Read your draft. Add: _____ two similes   _____ one personification

  _____ one more color   _____ one onomatopoeia

  Then: _____ change two "said" verbs

☐ 5. Make sure your first sentence is engaging and interesting.

☐ 6. Think of a title for your story that touches upon your main character and/or theme.

☐ 7. When your story is complete, plan it out on the **Storyboard: Children's Book**. Add illustrations that reflect the text that you wrote.

☐ 8. Create your book. Submit the book with your prewriting, drafts, and this sheet.

		Preliminary Grade	Revised Grade
Structure (book pages, length, title)	20%		
Process (questions, prewriting, drafts)	20%		
Ideas (setting, characters, plot, theme)	20%		
Language (images, simile, personification, onomatopoeia, no banned words or clichés)	20%		
Grammar/Spelling (punctuation, tenses, sentences, _____)	20%		
TOTAL			

Name _____ Date _____

Children's Book

Answer the following on a separate sheet of paper.

1. Who will be your main **character**?

2. Describe him/her fully.

   Animal or Person?   Age?

   Looks?   Clothes? Habits?

3. **Conflict:** What is the main character's problem? What does he/she want?

4. **Setting:** Where will the story take place?

Sights and Colors:	Sounds:
Smells:	Textures/Temperature/Weather:

5. Are there any other characters in the story, such as friends or family? Who are they?

6. **Point of View:** Who will tell your story—a character (which one?) or an outside narrator?

7. **Rising Action:** How will the main character try to solve the problem and get what he/she wants?

8. **Climax:** What finally works?

9. Does anything else happen after that? (This is the *falling action* and *resolution*.)

10. **Theme:** What will the main character *learn* or *realize*?

11. Summarize your story on a plot chart like the one below.

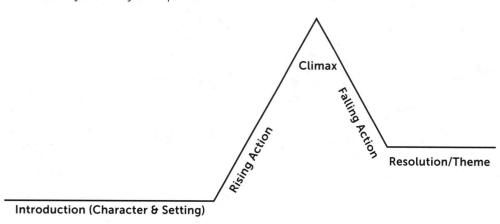

Name _____ Date _____

Living Legend

☐ 1. You will write a true story about an older person in your life, and you will write it in the first person, as if he/she were speaking. Read the sample legend and answer these prompts:

- Describe the main character—gender, age, job, traits, and so on.
- What does the main character want?
- Find five sensory details in the story.
- How does it feel to read this story in the first person?

☐ 2. Think of an older person in your life whom you could interview. Then think of 10 questions you could ask that person in order to find a story to write about. Fill out the **Prewriting Sheet: Living Legend Interview.**

☐ 3. Schedule an interview with the person. Use your interview questions until you find a single story to write about. **Do not try to write about his/her entire life.** Find a moment.

☐ 4. Take your notes about your story, and complete the **Prewriting Sheet: Short Story** as best you can. You may need to speak to your interviewee again to get more details.

☐ 5. Write (or type) a first draft of your story. Remember to write in first person *(I, me, we, us)*, as if you were the interviewee.

☐ 6. Make sure your story has a theme. Tell what the main character learned from this event.

☐ 7. Your story should be at least _____ page(s). Revise and add details. Upgrade four verbs and give the story an engaging title. Edit your work.

☐ 8. Submit your prewriting, drafts, final copy, and this sheet.

		Preliminary Grade	Revised Grade
Structure (paragraphs, length, title)	20%		
Process (questions, prewriting, drafts)	20%		
Ideas (setting, characters, details, theme)	20%		
Language (no banned words, clichés, wordiness)	20%		
Grammar/Spelling (punctuation, tenses, sentences, _____)	20%		
TOTAL			

50 Writing Activities for Meeting Higher Standards © Marilyn Pryle • Scholastic Inc

Name _____ Date _____

Living Legend Interview

Before you conduct your interview for this assignment, brainstorm 10 possible questions you can ask the person about his/her life. This will help you go into the interview prepared.

Sample questions could be: How did you meet your spouse? What is your funniest memory from school? What did it feel like to leave for war? What was your best memory growing up?

Person to Interview: _____

10 Possible Questions:

1.

2.

3.

4.

5.

6.

7.

8.

9.

10.

> **REMEMBER**
> This assignment is not meant to tell the person's entire life story; it is meant to focus on one moment or event in the person's life, and to tell that event fully with rich details.
>
> The questions you think of here are meant to help you find that one moment. Once you find it, focus on the details of that moment, and discard the rest of your questions.

Name _____ Date _____

Short Story

☐ 1. Read the short story provided, and answer the following prompts on paper:

- Who is the main character, and what does that character want?

- List five details about the character's looks or habits.

- List five details about the setting.

- What does the character realize or learn by the end? What is the theme?

- Who tells this story? What effect does that have on the reader?

☐ 2. You will write your own short story. Begin with the **Prewriting Sheet: Short Story Concept**.

☐ 3. When you have a basic idea for your story and for the structure of your story, complete the **Prewriting Sheet: Short Story**.

☐ 4. Write out a draft of your story. Aim for at least _____ page(s).

☐ 5. When you have a cohesive draft, revise. Upgrade at least four verbs. Give the piece a title, and edit your work.

☐ 6. Submit your prewriting, drafts, final copy, and this sheet.

		Preliminary Grade	Revised Grade
Structure (paragraphs, length, point of view, title)	20%		
Process (questions, prewriting, drafts)	20%		
Ideas (setting, characters, plot, details, theme)	20%		
Language (no banned words, clichés, wordiness)	20%		
Grammar/Spelling (punctuation, tenses, sentences, _____)	20%		
TOTAL			

     50 Writing Activities for Meeting Higher Standards © Marilyn Pryle • Scholastic Inc

Name _____ Date _____

Short Story Concept

1. All stories center around a character with a motivation. A motivation could be:

   - Something the character wants (a goal, an achievement, or something intangible like acceptance, love, or popularity)

   - Something the character wants to overcome (a disability or challenge, a loss, or something intangible, like prejudice, not being accepted, or a lack of self-confidence)

   - Dealing with a situation that has been put upon the character (an unwanted loss or accident, or a big change or move)

   Another way to look at motivation is to think of it as the story's **conflict** (or **problem**).

   Brainstorm below who your **main character** could be and what his/her main **motivation** or **conflict** could be for this story.

Possible Characters (Give gender, age, situation)	Possible Motivation or Conflict

2. **Character:** Choose *one* of these scenarios and star it. This will be the basis for your story. (As you write, you can make changes as new ideas come to you—but always be sure you have a main character with a motivation.)

3. **Plot:** On another sheet, plot out a possible story. For now, focus only on main events. You can use one of the following structures to map out your summary:

   a) paragraph or list   b) plot chart   c) storyboard

4. **Point of View:** Who will tell this story—the main character, a minor character, or an outside narrator? Why do you think this is the best choice for your story?

5. Complete the **Prewriting Sheet: Short Story** to plan out your story even more.

Name _____ Date _____

Historical Fiction

☐ 1. **Historical fiction** is a made-up story based on true events that happened in history. The characters, for example, may be fictional, but the events and places are not. Or, the characters may have been real people, but the writer fills in some dialogue and action in between the important events. List four books or movies you have read which can be classified as historical fiction.

☐ 2. Read the sample piece of historical fiction. Answer the following prompts on paper:

   • Name five details from this piece that are historically true.

   • Name five details from this piece that are fictional.

   • Is the narration in first or third person? What is the effect of that choice?

   • Give three sensory details about a character and three about the setting.

☐ 3. Choose a historical event or person to write about. Complete the **Research Sheet: Historical Fiction**.

☐ 4. Complete the **Prewriting Sheet: Short Story Concept**.

☐ 5. Complete the **Prewriting Sheet: Short Story**.

☐ 6. Write your draft. Remember that historical fiction is rooted in fact. You cannot change any major dates, names, or places that already exist in history. Continue to research as needed while you are writing. Aim for at least _____ page(s).

☐ 7. When you have a cohesive draft, revise. Upgrade at least four verbs. Give the piece a title, and edit your work.

☐ 8. Submit your prewriting, drafts, final copy, and this sheet.

		Preliminary Grade	Revised Grade
Structure (paragraphs, length, point of view, title)	20%		
Process (questions, prewriting, drafts)	20%		
Ideas (setting, characters, details, plot, theme)	20%		
Language (no banned words, clichés, wordiness)	20%		
Grammar/Spelling (punctuation, tenses, sentences, _____)	20%		
TOTAL			

50 Writing Activities for Meeting Higher Standards © Marilyn Pryle • Scholastic In

Name _____ Date _____

Historical Fiction

Historical event or person that will be the basis of your story:

_____

Research your topic and list several facts in the categories below, citing your sources.
Use the back of this sheet if you need more space.

Category	Facts/Details	Source(s)
Possible Setting		
Clothes		
Technology		
Transportation		
Furniture		
Hair/Jewelry/ Personal Belongings		
Food		

Expository Writing

Expository writing includes description, explanation, classification, reflection, and some analysis. (Note that in this book, I have put formal "analysis" essays in the Persuasive block of activities, since I've required them to have a claim.) Although expository writing is not narrative, it can still be about the writer's life and interests—many of the activities here ask students to write about what they know; often, they will be the experts in their topics. The following exercises will help students learn valuable expository skills while looking closely at their lives and the world around them. The Writing Assignments and Prewriting Sheets start on page 60, and the writing models are online; see page 127. At right are the relevant standards for expository writing.

MAIN STANDARD

Write descriptive, informative, and reflective texts to examine and communicate detailed information clearly and in an organized way.

ADDITIONAL STANDARDS

▶ Generate cohesive pieces focusing on the assignment, purpose, and audience.

▶ Participate in the writing process (reading, prewriting, drafting, revising, and editing).

▶ Demonstrate a clear understanding of the conventions of English.

▶ Demonstrate an ability to use effective figurative language and appropriate vocabulary depending on assignment, purpose, and audience.

21 Introduce Yourself!

This is a wonderful activity for the beginning of the year. The focus of this activity is organization—taking ideas and sorting them into paragraphs. For model writing, write a letter to the students about yourself. Brainstorm ideas about your life, and model how you put those ideas into groups to create paragraphs. When reading your letter, have students recognize the main idea in each paragraph. You will also need to instruct students about setting up a letter with a return address, recipient's address, date, greeting, body, and closing.

22 What's in a Name?

This fun activity has the topic built in! Students must weave together a bit of autobiography, research, family history, and opinion in the piece. If desired, this could be an apt opportunity to demonstrate how an opinion is used in an expository way instead of a persuasive way. An additional mini-lesson could be about citing sources. As with other activities, brainstorming for the introduction appears last. The model writing is available online as Resource 22.3; see page 127 for instructions on how to access.

MULTIMEDIA IDEA

Create a Wikibook of the students' names and their origins.

23 Me, in Metaphors

This descriptive poetry-writing assignment asks students to think of personality traits and talents and translate those into metaphors. This activity would also be fun for the beginning of the year; it could even be used as an anonymous ice-breaker game as students try to match poems with their authors. Additionally, finished poems could be collected into a class anthology or posted to the class website, with student photos alongside them. The model writing is available online as Resource 23.3; see page 127 for instructions on how to access.

24 Epic Hero Shield and Reflection

Focusing on the elements of the epic hero, this assignment does double duty! The archetype of the hero is present in many texts, regardless of curriculum or culture. Students must view their own lives through the lens of the hero, create a collage in the form of a shield, and write a reflection. Visual examples of shields are invaluable here, and you might want to limit the size to 12-by-14 inches or smaller. For the "hero's flaws" section, I usually steer students to consider what challenges them, such as time management, motivation, or specific fears; I don't push them to focus on their own personality flaws per se.

FOLLOW-UP ACTIVITY

I usually do the shield project at the start of the year, and keep the shields after they have been displayed. At the end of the year, I have students write another reflection about how the shields have changed or remained the same.

Another note: Many students will claim they "don't have a motto." Assure them that now is a perfect time to think of one. For the reflection, I've found that more focused questions (such as the ones listed) yield more in-depth writing. If students are simply asked to "reflect on their shield," they often end up merely listing, in sentences, the pictures they've put on it. I leave the finished shields on display for some time, since students find one another's projects both interesting and inspirational.

25 Classify Your Crib

This classification essay focuses on brainstorming and forming groups that will be shaped into paragraphs. Students should have plenty of ideas since they use their own rooms as topics. For a conclusion, students are asked to do some inferencing: What do these objects and groups say about you? (Note: There purposefully is no sample essay for this assignment because students should practice naming their own groups [i.e., classifying]. When you present this exercise to the class, resist giving them group names, such as "sports equipment," "video game materials," or "furniture." Let students figure out how to classify.)

26 Process Essay

Students use their talents, hobbies, or jobs as topics for the Process Essay. This exercise emphasizes how writers can take the conclusion an extra step beyond summarizing (see page 18 about writing conclusions), as well as sequencing and using transition words. Appropriate mini-lessons would include transition words of addition or sequence, introductions, and conclusions. The model writing is available online as Resource 26.3; see page 127 for instructions on how to access.

MULTIMEDIA IDEA
Students can present their Process Essays live, or as videos, demonstrating the process.

27 Ode

This free-verse poem praising something can be about anything, but if your class is doing the Setting Sketch and Character Sketch, I suggest you have students write their odes about a thing (tangible or intangible) for variety. The assignment reinforces sensory details as well as a basic idea of theme, and requires students to practice literary techniques, such as using personification, onomatopoeia, and similes. For more examples, look to Pablo Neruda's many odes or the book *Neighborhood Odes* by Gary Soto (2005). The model writing is available online as Resource 27.3; see page 127 for instructions on how to access.

PUBLICATION IDEA
Gather all odes into a class book, or post to the class blog.

28 Thank-You Letter

The main idea of a Thank-You Letter is "I am grateful to you," and this idea is supported by facts and reasons. It is also an effective activity to introduce purpose and audience, since these are so clear-cut. (In a thank-you letter, the purpose is often in the very first sentence.) Mini-lessons could be about employing a letter format and addressing envelopes. These letters should be actually mailed, or at least sent via email. For a sample letter, I encourage you to write your own thank-you letter to someone and share it with students. This will increase the level of trust and authenticity in your class. The model writing is available online as Resource 28.3; see page 127 for instructions on how to access.

29 Compare and Contrast Essay

On the assignment sheet, students are asked to find their own topics that they know a lot about. However, this assignment can be repeated with assigned topics or topics related to readings, if desired. A fitting mini-lesson would be about using contrasting transition words. The two possible structures for this essay are included on the Prewriting Sheet and may also need to be reviewed in a whole-class setting. The T-Chart and model writing are available online as Resources 29.3 and 29.4; see page 127 for instructions on how to access.

FOLLOW-UP IDEAS
After students write the Break Up With a Bad Habit letter, have them formulate a concrete plan or timeline for taking steps to overcome the habit.

If this assignment is done earlier in the year, save the letters and give them back at the end of the year. Students can reflect on any progress they've made with the habit!

30 Break Up With a Bad Habit

I encourage you to write your own sample for this exercise; if we constantly expect students to be open and truthful with us, we must model being appropriately open and truthful with them. I like to tell students that adults struggle in many of the same ways they do, and that being strong and determined is a lifelong practice. Choose something that's true for you but would resonate with students, such as procrastinating, not speaking up, or eating junk food. You might even want to give students some small-group time to discuss some possible topics. This activity focuses on author's purpose and paragraphing. The model writing is available online as Resource 30.3; see page 127 for instructions on how to access.

31 School Survival Guide

This fun essay is another version of a Process Essay. For examples, circulate actual copies of the Worst-Case Scenario Survival Handbook series, a collection of books that gives step-by-step instructions for surviving scenarios such as snakebites and volcanic eruptions. Note that the structure of those pieces are a mix of paragraphs, lists, and illustrations. Students will enjoy experimenting with this format.

32 News Account

Although the practice of the "5 Ws" is an old one, it is more important now than ever in our modern age of persuasion and opinion. Having students report only the facts without inserting their feelings is a valuable skill. For a model, use an actual news story from your local paper; choose one with a few sensory details. You may want to do a prewriting exercise about distinguishing fact from opinion.

33 Passion Pursuit

Students will write a short, inquiry-based research paper on the topic of their choice. They will need much help in narrowing down their areas of interest to manageable topics, and they will also need help citing sources and learning how not to plagiarize. Students should have some experience with writing introductions and conclusions before attempting this activity, and they can consult their notes for help. If you haven't yet done a mini-lesson on titles, you will have the opportunity here. Remind students that the assignment is factual and their purpose is to inform; they should not include any opinions, and their main topic should clearly appear by the end of the introduction. The assignment can be shortened or lengthened as desired. If you choose to make this a longer paper, you may want to give more detailed instruction on either MLA or APA formatting. Finally, the Prewriting Sheet instructs students to make a web to explore their topics; you could do a longer lesson on mind mapping, and even assign a more formal mind map as part of the activity—many sites such as coggle.it and mindmeister.com offer free mind-mapping programs.

34 Ponder the Progress

This personal reflection is powerful for the end of each quarter or the first semester—after some time has passed, but while some time still remains to improve. Emphasize to students that there are no right answers to the questions on the Prewriting Sheet—the only requirement is effort and sincere thought. You may also want to reassure students that you will be the only reader of the reflection, if that is your choice; they may be more willing to reflect honestly. To take the assignment a step further, you could save any reflections done throughout the year and at the end of the year, have students write a final reflection in which they examine their overall growth.

MULTIMEDIA IDEAS

Give each student, or pairs of students, different survival topics, and publish all the scenarios as a Wikibook.

Publish all the news stories as an online newspaper in Google Blogger.

MULTIMEDIA SPEAKING IDEA

Have students transform their news stories into presentations, which they can deliver live or record as a video.

MIND MAP IT

Many sites offer free mind mapping tools that can help students explore their topics and give examples of how to ask questions about a topic.

Name _____ Date _____

Introduce Yourself!

☐ 1. Read the letter I have written to you. In the margin of my letter, write the main idea for each paragraph. You are going to write a letter back to me.

☐ 2. On paper, brainstorm any ideas about yourself that you want me to know. Be specific.

☐ 3. Organize the information into groups. You should be putting together ideas for three or four paragraphs. (Note: Some of your ideas may not fit into any paragraph's main idea. If you still want them for your letter, add ideas to them to make a new paragraph.)

☐ 4. Number the groups in the order that seems best: Which do you want to tell first, second, and third?

☐ 5. Write a first draft. Be sure to use a letter format (see my example) that includes a **recipient address**, a **sender's address**, and a **date**.

☐ 6. Read it and revise it—look for places where you can add some description (sights, sounds, smells, textures, and so on). Edit your work. It should be at least _____ page(s).

☐ 7. Submit your prewriting, drafts, final copy, and this sheet.

· ·

		Preliminary Grade	Revised Grade
Structure (letter format, paragraphs, length)	20%		
Process (prewriting, editing, drafts)	20%		
Ideas (1 main idea per paragraph, details)	20%		
Language (no banned words, clichés, wordiness)	20%		
Grammar/Spelling (punctuation, tenses, sentences, _____)	20%		
TOTAL			

50 Writing Activities for Meeting Higher Standards © Marilyn Pryle • Scholastic Inc

Name _____ Date _____

What's in a Name?

☐ 1. Read the model writing. Answer the following questions:

- What technique does the writer use for an introduction?

- What are the facts about the author's name?

- What technique does the author use for a conclusion?

☐ 2. You will write a short personal essay about your own name. Complete the
Prewriting Sheet: What's in a Name?

☐ 3. Write a draft, using the format in the model as your guide. Have four paragraphs:

- An introduction, using a short "everyday" moment with sensory details

- A facts paragraph about your name, using your research

- A paragraph explaining how you got your name and any special meaning

- A conclusion, in which you give your opinion about your name

☐ 4. After you have a draft, read and revise it. Edit your work. Give the piece a title.
It should be at least _____ page(s).

☐ 5. Submit your prewriting, drafts, final copy, and this sheet.

		Preliminary Grade	Revised Grade
Structure (length, paragraphs, order, title)	20%		
Process (prewriting, editing, drafts)	20%		
Ideas (1 main idea per paragraph, research, citations, details)	20%		
Language (no banned words, clichés, wordiness)	20%		
Grammar/Spelling (punctuation, tenses, sentences, _____)	20%		
TOTAL			

Name _____ Date _____

What's in a Name?

Topic: Your first name: _____

Research: Find information about your name; continue this chart on the back if needed.

Topic	Information	Source
Culture(s) of Origin		
Literal Meaning/ Meaning of Roots		
Famous People with the Same Name		
Popularity in Different Eras		

Family Meaning: Is there any special meaning to your name within your family? Were you named after someone? Did someone important name you? How was your name chosen?

Conclusion: How do you feel about your name? Why?

Introduction: Can you think of an everyday moment involving your name—for example, when your parent, sibling, or friend usually says your name? Do you have a nickname or short version of your name? Write out a scenario; use at least **three** sensory details.

    50 Writing Activities for Meeting Higher Standards © Marilyn Pryle • Scholastic Inc

Name _____ Date _____

Me, in Metaphors

☐ 1. You will write a poem describing yourself, using only metaphors. Remember that a **metaphor** is a comparison that does NOT use *like* or *as*. For example: "The cafeteria is an ant farm full of movement and alliances."

☐ 2. Complete the **Prewriting Sheet: Me, in Metaphors**. You can use images from nature, human-made objects, sports, history, art, and so on. The first one is an example.

☐ 3. Write your poem, adding and revising as you do. You can begin each sentence with "I am" or you can use another subject, such as "My mind is the silent, gray stone at the bottom of a noisy river." Break the lines of your poem wherever it seems natural.

☐ 4. Put the images in any order you want. Your last image should be your most powerful one, giving the reader something to think about at the end.

☐ 5. Think of a clever or engaging title for this poem. Maybe one of the images could work.

☐ 6. Read your poem and revise it. Then edit your work.

☐ 7. Submit your prewriting, drafts, final copy, and this sheet.

		Preliminary Grade	Revised Grade
Structure (length, poem format, title)	20%		
Process (prewriting, editing, drafts)	20%		
Ideas (8 metaphors, sensory details)	20%		
Language (no banned words, clichés, wordiness)	20%		
Grammar/Spelling (punctuation, tenses, sentences, _____)	20%		
TOTAL			

Name _____ Date _____

Me, in Metaphors

Think of eight qualities about yourself (these could be physical, emotional, mental) or talents that you have. List them. Think of an image (sight, sound, smell, taste, or texture) that could represent that quality. Then add to that image to make it interesting and descriptive.

Quality	Basic Image	Image with More Description
peaceful	stones in a river	gray, black, and speckled stones that lie at the bottom of a noisy river

Now, look at your last column. Add some **alliteration**, **onomatopoeia**, or **personification** to each image.

Name _____ Date _____

Epic Hero Shield and Reflection

Part 1: Shield

☐ 1. Think of a movie or book (often part of a series) that contains an epic hero. Usually, the archetype of the epic hero has certain characteristics. On paper, give details about these characteristics of your chosen epic hero.

- The hero's narrative or backstory (may include family, hometown, childhood)
- The hero's characteristics (his/her strong qualities, with evidence)
- The hero's flaws (his/her weakness, especially character traits or personal challenges)
- The hero's quests (goals, desires, outer challenges)
- Does this hero live by a motto or saying? Is there a moment in the story in which someone speaks a line that encapsulates the strengths or the cause of the hero? Write it.

☐ 2. Throughout history, shields have been used not only for protection but for identification. A hero's crest or symbol may appear on the shield. You will create a shield about yourself and your own life. For this assignment, YOU are the hero, and your life is the epic tale. Complete the **Brainstorming Sheet: Epic Hero Shield**.

☐ 3. Find pictures or symbols to represent each of your ideas on the brainstorming sheet. The motto does not need pictures.

☐ 4. On a piece of poster board or heavy paper, arrange and decorate your shield. You can use any style, but make sure the categories are clear. The motto can be placed anywhere.

☐ 5. Put your name and class on the back and submit your shield.

		Preliminary Grade	Revised Grade
Structure (shield shape, clear categories, effort)	10%		
Narrative Section (4 pictures x 5 points each)	20%		
Qualities Section (4 pictures x 5 points each)	20%		
Flaws Section (4 pictures x 5 points each)	20%		
Quest Section (4 pictures x 5 points each)	20%		
Motto	10%		
TOTAL			

Name _____ Date _____

Epic Hero Shield

Your shield will have five sections of pictures and symbols. Brainstorm some ideas for each section; have a minimum of four for each section, except the motto, which is simply a saying.

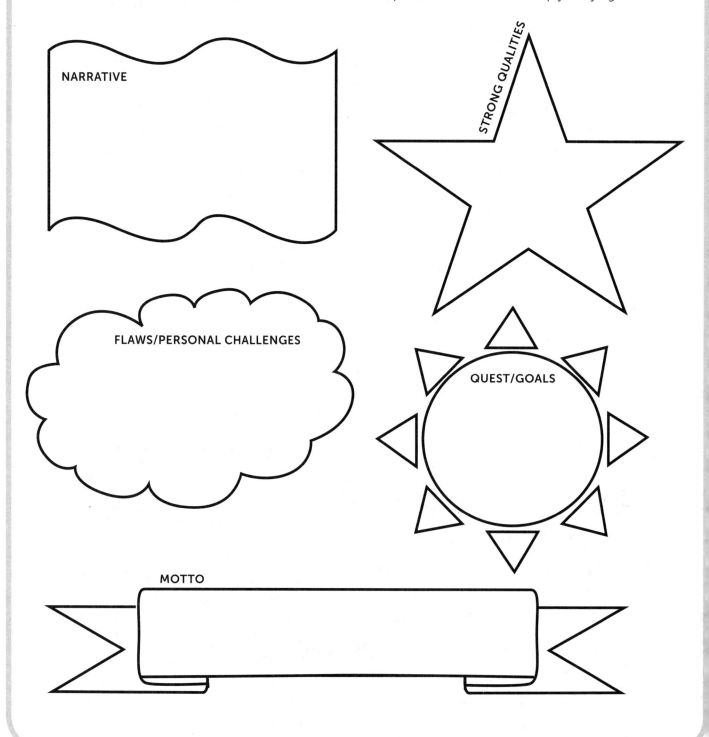

50 Writing Activities for Meeting Higher Standards © Marilyn Pryle • Scholastic Inc

Name _____ Date _____

Epic Hero Shield and Reflection

Part 2: Reflection

- [ ] 1. You will write a reflection about some aspect of your shield. Choose **one** of the following questions, and brainstorm some ideas for your chosen question on paper.

    - Which of these sections motivates you the most? How? Why? (Choose one section only.)

    - Is there a story behind your motto? What is it? Why did you choose your motto? What does it remind you of? Explain how/when you think of it (and give an example).

    - Imagine a day in your life without your "hero's flaws." What would that day be like? Describe it. How would it feel to live like this? What are three small actions you could take now to bring you a little bit closer to that imaginary day?

    - Explain your quest (or one part of it). What exactly will it take to attain it? What will it feel like once you have attained it? Imagine that moment and describe it.

    - Look at your "flaws" section. What other sections or symbols on your shield balance out the flaws? How? How could these other parts help you eventually overcome your flaws?

- [ ] 2. Write up your reflection. Be sure you have a purposeful beginning and ending. Your reflection should be _____ page(s).

- [ ] 3. Read what you have. Revise and edit. Upgrade four verbs. Give the essay a title.

- [ ] 4. Submit your prewriting, drafts, final copy, and this sheet.

		Preliminary Grade	Revised Grade
Structure (length, paragraphs, title)	20%		
Process (prewriting, editing, drafts)	20%		
Ideas (1 main idea per paragraph, details/examples)	20%		
Language (no banned words, clichés, wordiness)	20%		
Grammar/Spelling (punctuation, tenses, sentences, _____)	20%		
TOTAL			

Name _____ Date _____

Classify Your Crib

☐ 1. Think of your room at home. What's in it? Think of objects but also details (colors, sounds, smells, and textures). Brainstorm a list on the **Prewriting Sheet: Classify Your Crib**.

☐ 2. Look at your list. Do you see any patterns or groups that you could form? Group your items and give each group a name. You may add or subtract items from your original list as you group. If you have any leftover items that you think are important, you could create a final group called "Miscellaneous Items."

☐ 3. Look at your groups. What do these groups and items say about you? What could a stranger infer from this list? On the back of your sheet, write a few sentences about how these items reveal your hobbies, values, personality, and family.

☐ 4. Write an essay describing your room, using your groups as paragraphs.

For an **introduction**, use sensory details and give the first impression one would get when entering your room.

For a **conclusion**, use your answer to #3 about what your room says about you.

☐ 5. After you have a draft, read your essay and revise it. Give it a title, and edit your work. The essay should be at least _____ page(s).

☐ 6. Submit your prewriting, drafts, final copy, and this sheet.

		Preliminary Grade	Revised Grade
Structure (length, paragraphs, title)	20%		
Process (prewriting, editing, drafts)	20%		
Ideas (1 main idea per paragraph, details, conclusion)	20%		
Language (no banned words, clichés, wordiness)	20%		
Grammar/Spelling (punctuation, tenses, sentences, _____)	20%		
TOTAL			

Name _____ Date _____

Classify Your Crib

(Continue on back if needed.)

Brainstorm (objects, colors, sounds, smells, textures)	**Groups** Categorize your list; be sure to give each group a title.

1.
2.
3.
4.
5.
6.
7.
8.
9.
10.
11.
12.
13.
14.
15.
16.
17.
18.
19.
20.
21.
22.
23.
24.
25.
26.
27.
28.
29.
30.

Name _____ Date _____

Process Essay

☐ 1. Read the sample essay and answer the following on a separate sheet of paper.

- What technique does the author use for an introduction?

- Is the process described in order? Number the steps.

- Find two sensory details.

- Does the author take the conclusion one step further? How?

☐ 2. Think about some process that you know how to do. It should be something you care about and you think is important. Complete the **Prewriting Sheet: Process Essay**.

☐ 3. Add details to your steps—colors, shapes, sounds, smells, textures, tastes.

☐ 4. Write up a draft. It should be at least _____ page(s).

☐ 5. Make sure your conclusion goes the extra step. Use your ideas in the "Theme" section. Make sure the introduction will grab the reader's attention.

☐ 6. Read the draft. Ask yourself these questions, and then revise:

- Are the steps in the proper order?

- Can I add some transition words (*first, then, next, finally*)?

- Do I define any words my readers might not understand? Do I give background information?

☐ 7. Edit your draft. Upgrade four verbs. Think of a title.

☐ 8. Submit your prewriting, drafts, final copy, and this sheet.

		Preliminary Grade	Revised Grade
Structure (length, paragraphs, title)	20%		
Process (prewriting, editing, drafts)	20%		
Ideas (clear steps, transitions, theme)	20%		
Language (no banned words, clichés, wordiness)	20%		
Grammar/Spelling (punctuation, tenses, sentences, _____)	20%		
TOTAL			

Name _____ Date _____

Process Essay

Process you know well: _____

Steps	Sensory Details
1.	
2.	
3.	
4.	
5.	
6.	
7.	
8.	

Theme: Why is this process, hobby, sport, etc., important? How has it helped you grow? What can a person learn about life through this process?

Intro: What could be an attention-grabbing introduction? Can you pick out some details to create a scene? Can you ask the reader an engaging question? Can you give a fact or statistic about your process? Jot down an idea here:

Name _____ Date _____

Ode

☐ 1. An **ode** is a poem that praises something or someone. To *praise* means "to express admiration for" or "to tell the positive qualities of."

☐ 2. Read the sample odes. Notice the colors, sights, sounds, textures, and smells. Answer the questions given.

☐ 3. Your ode will be about a thing. It can be about an everyday item, a special gift or possession, something in nature, something you made, an abstract idea (like love or childhood)—anything.

☐ 4. Write out your ideas on the **Prewriting Sheet: Ode**.

☐ 5. Write a first draft of your ode. You can use short lines or long lines.

☐ 6. Make sure you have at least **two similes and one instance of personification**. Try **one metaphor** and some **onomatopoeia**. For an ending, communicate what the topic means to you. This is your **theme**.

☐ 7. Revise your draft. Add **three more sensory details**, and make sure you have a title. Edit your work. Your ode should be at least _____ page(s).

☐ 8. Submit your prewriting, drafts, final copy, and this sheet.

		Preliminary Grade	Revised Grade
Structure (length, poem format, title)	20%		
Process (prewriting, editing, drafts)	20%		
Ideas (sensory details, similes, personification, onomatopoeia, metaphor)	20%		
Language (no banned words, clichés, wordiness)	20%		
Grammar/Spelling (punctuation, tenses, sentences, _____)	20%		
TOTAL			

Name _____ Date _____

Ode

Choose a topic for your ode. It could be a special gift, an everyday item, something in nature, an abstract idea, or something else. It can be outside or indoors, big or small. Write your topic here:

Topic: _____

Now, imagine it for a few minutes and fill out the chart below. This will be your brainstorming.

Sights (shape, size, characteristics, etc.)	Colors Smells
Touch (textures, temperature)	Sounds
Personification (What does it do that is like a person's actions?)	Onomatopoeia (look above at "Sounds")
Similes (description using *like* or *as*)	Metaphor
Memories of the Topic	Daily Routines Involving the Topic

Why did you choose this topic? What does it mean to you? Write your answer on the back.

Name _____ Date _____

Thank-You Letter

☐ 1. A thank-you letter expresses your gratitude to someone and explains why you are grateful. Read the model thank-you letter and answer the following questions:

- To whom is the writer thankful?

- What is the main thing (topic) the writer is grateful for?

- What are the specific reasons for this?

- How does the writer conclude the letter?

☐ 2. Complete the **Prewriting Sheet: Thank-You Letter**.

☐ 3. Write your letter. Your letter can have three paragraphs:

- an intro that contains the main purpose/focus

- a body paragraph with specific reasons and details

- a conclusion that reiterates your gratitude and uses an *if/then* sentence

☐ 4. Be sure to also have a **return address, date, greeting,** a **closing,** and a **signature**.

☐ 5. Read over the letter and revise. When ready, edit. It should be at least _____ page(s).

☐ 6. Submit your prewriting, drafts, final copy, and this sheet.

		Preliminary Grade	Revised Grade
Structure (letter format, paragraphs, length)	20%		
Process (prewriting, editing, drafts)	20%		
Ideas (clear topic, specific reasons, details, conclusion)	20%		
Language (no banned words, clichés, wordiness)	20%		
Grammar/Spelling (punctuation, tenses, sentences, _____)	20%		
TOTAL			

50 Writing Activities for Meeting Higher Standards © Marilyn Pryle • Scholastic Inc.

Name _____ Date _____

Thank-You Letter

1. **Recipient:** Write some names of people you are grateful to at this time:

   Now, circle one you feel you could write a letter to, expressing your gratitude.

2. **Topic:** What exactly are you grateful for? Try to be specific. What action(s) did the person do for you? Or, was there a specific event that took place? Write down some ideas below, and then choose one to be the focus/purpose of the letter.

3. **Reasons:** Why are you grateful for the person's actions? Think of at least two or three reasons, and give details and further information about each.

Reasons	Additional Info, Backstory, or Sensory Details
1.	
2.	
3.	

4. **Conclusion:** What would have happened (or not happened) if the person didn't help you the way he/she did? Try a sentence with an *if/then* structure (*If you hadn't practiced pitching with me each day, then our team would not have made it to the finals*). Try not to repeat something from #3. Write your conclusion on the back.

Name _____ Date _____

Compare and Contrast Essay

☐ 1. Read the sample essay and answer the following on a separate sheet of paper.

- What organizational technique did the writer use?

- What technique did the writer use for an introduction?

- What technique did the writer use for a conclusion?

- List three transition words in the piece.

☐ 2. Choose two topics (people, places, objects, animals, sports, etc.) to compare and contrast. Choose topics you are interested in and know a lot about. Look through your "Life List" for help.

☐ 3. Complete the **Prewriting Sheet: Compare and Contrast Essay**.

☐ 4. Write a first draft. Review your notes on transition words, introductions, and conclusions.

☐ 5. Revise the draft. Check for:　_____ a title

_____ an attention-grabbing introduction

_____ a strong conclusion

_____ at least four transition words

☐ 6. Reread the essay and revise again. Edit your work. It should be at least _____ page(s).

☐ 7. Submit your prewriting, drafts, final copy, and this sheet.

		Preliminary Grade	Revised Grade
Structure (length, organization, title)	20%		
Process (prewriting, editing, drafts)	20%		
Ideas (1 main idea per paragraph, transitions, quality of intro/conclusion)	20%		
Language (no banned words, clichés, wordiness)	20%		
Grammar/Spelling (punctuation, tenses, sentences, _____)	20%		
TOTAL			

50 Writing Activities for Meeting Higher Standards © Marilyn Pryle • Scholastic Inc.

Name _____ Date _____

Compare and Contrast Essay

1. Two topics to be compared:

2. On a T-Chart, brainstorm a list of qualities for each. The list does not have to match up on each side—just write down any ideas that you have about each topic.

3. What would be the best way to organize your ideas? Circle one of the possibilities below:

    By Topic

    1. Introduction

    2. Topic #1: all characteristics

    3. Topic #2: all characteristics

    4. Conclusion

    By Characteristic

    1. Introduction

    2. Characteristic #1: both topics

    3. Characteristic #2: both topics

    4. Characteristic #3: both topics

    5. Conclusion

4. Below the T-Chart, organize your ideas from your list into paragraphs, using the organizational structure you chose.

5. What would make an engaging introduction? Can you create a scene with sensory details, use a statistic, or ask an interesting and detailed question? Try some ideas below:

6. Think about your conclusion. Can you do anything else besides summarize? Could you give an opinion, tell why your topic is important, or return to the scene you created in the intro? Try some ideas on the back.

Name _____ Date _____

Break Up With a Bad Habit

☐ 1. Read the sample letter. In the margin of the letter, write the main idea for each paragraph. You are also going to write a break-up letter to a habit you want to leave behind. You will address the habit in the second person, as if it were an actual recipient.

☐ 2. Complete the **Prewriting Sheet: Break Up With a Bad Habit**.

☐ 3. Write your letter. Be sure to have a **return address, date, greeting** (such as "Dear Procrastination"), the **four paragraphs from the Prewriting Sheet,** a **closing,** and a **signature**.

☐ 4. Read it and revise it—look for places where you can add some description (sights, sounds, smells, textures, etc.).

☐ 5. Reread the letter and revise again. Edit your work. It should be at least _____ page(s).

☐ 6. Submit your prewriting, drafts, final copy, and this sheet.

		Preliminary Grade	Revised Grade
Structure (letter format, paragraphs, length)	20%		
Process (prewriting, editing, drafts)	20%		
Ideas (1 main idea per paragraph, details, motto)	20%		
Language (no banned words, clichés, wordiness)	20%		
Grammar/Spelling (punctuation, tenses, sentences, _____)	20%		
TOTAL			

50 Writing Activities for Meeting Higher Standards © Marilyn Pryle • Scholastic Inc.

Name _____ Date _____

Break Up With a Bad Habit

What is the habit you want to "break up" with? _____

Brainstorm some ideas for each of the following sections:

1. **Introduction:** State the purpose of the letter in the first sentence, and describe your "history" with the habit. You could even retell a specific incident. Jot down ideas and details here:

2. **Reason Paragraph #1:** Tell why you want to stop the habit. Explain all the problems or suffering it has caused you. Brainstorm here:

3. **Reason Paragraph #2:** Imagine your life without the habit. What would it be like? Describe a day or week without the habit dogging you.

4. **Conclusion:** Reiterate the purpose of the letter. Write a vow to drop the habit starting today. Write an affirmation of the new qualities you will embrace instead of the habit. End your letter telling the habit of a new motto you will use to remind yourself to be strong. Write your ideas here:

Name _____ Date _____

School Survival Guide

☐ 1. Browse through a "survival guide" in either book form or online. Answer the following:
- How are the chapters/selections structured?
- What person is the writing in (first, second, or third)?
- What is the person and audience of the piece?
- Are there any visuals? What do they show, and how do they help?

☐ 2. You will create a chapter for a survival guide about school. Think of a narrow topic that you can explain. Here are some ideas:

- a certain class
- the bathroom
- the principal's office
- the cafeteria
- the hallway
- any sport
- homework
- homeroom
- recess
- a sport bus
- the gym
- the bus

☐ 3. Keep your topic narrow and think of every detail surrounding it. Complete the **Prewriting Sheet: School Survival Guide**.

☐ 4. Write your draft, using clear formatting for this genre:
- Number your steps/rules and **boldface** the first sentence of each.
- Each step should be its own paragraph.
- You should still have an introduction paragraph and a conclusion.
- Leave space for your visual.

☐ 5. Reread your draft and revise. Edit your work. The piece should be at least _____ page(s).

☐ 6. Submit your prewriting, drafts, final copy, and this sheet.

		Preliminary Grade	Revised Grade
Structure (length, paragraphs, list, title)	20%		
Process (prewriting, editing, drafts)	20%		
Ideas (clear steps, transitions, theme, visual)	20%		
Language (no banned words, clichés, wordiness)	20%		
Grammar/Spelling (punctuation, tenses, sentences, _____)	20%		
TOTAL			

    50 Writing Activities for Meeting Higher Standards © Marilyn Pryle • Scholastic Inc

Name _____ Date _____

School Survival Guide

1. **Topic:** What topic will you write about?

2. **Steps:** List the steps/rules to surviving your topic. For each step, give three sensory details. Use the back of this sheet if necessary.

Steps/Rules	Sensory Details
1.	
2.	
3.	
4.	
5.	
6.	

3. **Visual:** Think of a visual aid that could accompany your piece. It could be a drawing, diagram, chart, or photograph. It should somehow help the reader understand your meaning better. Write down an idea, and sketch it on the back of this sheet.

4. **Theme:** Why is this process important? What can the reader gain if your advice is followed? What could the reader lose if mistakes are made? Brainstorm some ideas below:

Name _____   Date _____

News Account

1. A news account should contain only the facts of a situation; the reader should not see any trace of the journalist's opinion or feelings. Read the sample news account and answer the following:

   - List the 5 Ws in this story (who, what, when, where, and why).
   - How does the piece begin? What is the starting technique?
   - How does the piece end?
   - Find three sensory details.
   - What is the tone of this story? Why, do you think?
   - What is the headline? How does it relate to the story?

2. Think of a current event that has happened recently. It could be something in school or in your town; it could be major or minor. It could even be something at home. Complete the **Prewriting Sheet: News Account**.

3. Draft your story. Reread the model to get ideas about the beginning, middle, and end. Notice the length of the paragraphs. After writing, try a headline.

4. Read what you have. Be sure you've included facts only, sensory details, and a headline. Revise. Upgrade four verbs.

5. Reread your draft and revise again. Edit your work. The piece should be at least _____ page(s).

6. Submit your prewriting, drafts, final copy, and this sheet.

		Preliminary Grade	Revised Grade
Structure (length, paragraphs, headline)	20%		
Process (prewriting, editing, drafts)	20%		
Ideas (facts only, 5 Ws, sensory details)	20%		
Language (no banned words, clichés, wordiness)	20%		
Grammar/Spelling (punctuation, tenses, sentences, _____)	20%		
TOTAL			

   50 Writing Activities for Meeting Higher Standards © Marilyn Pryle • Scholastic Inc

Name _____ Date _____

News Account

1. Brainstorm some events that have happened recently in your school, community, and home. These could be major (your school won the state championships) or minor (your family got a new dog). Write at least five ideas below:

2. Choose one of the ideas above and circle it. Below, list the "5 Ws" of the story. You may have to do some research outside of class.

   Who:

   What:

   When:

   Where:

   Why:

3. Look at your facts, and think of at least **three additional sensory details** that will make this story more vivid to the reader. (Be careful not to stray into "opinion" territory.)

4. What would make a clear, engaging **headline** for this story? Keep it factual.

Name _____ Date _____

Passion Pursuit

☐ 1. For this activity, you will do some research about a topic you are very interested in. Complete questions #1–2 on the **Prewriting Sheet: Passion Pursuit**.

☐ 2. The most important first step is to narrow your topic so that you will examine one small angle on it. Complete questions #3–6 on the Prewriting Sheet; get approval from your teacher.

☐ 3. Conduct your research (#7) and keep track of all your information and sources.

☐ 4. Plan and write your paper (#8–10). Revise as you write until you have a complete draft.

 This piece should be at least _____ page(s).

☐ 5. Read the paper, and revise again. Be sure you have the following:

 _____ an appealing title   _____ cited quotes and paraphrasing

 _____ an engaging intro   _____ an interesting conclusion

 _____ the topic in the first paragraph   _____ a citations page

 _____ logical paragraphs   _____ page numbers

☐ 6. Edit your work.

☐ 7. Submit your prewriting, drafts, final copy, and this sheet.

		Preliminary Grade	Revised Grade
Structure (length, paragraphs, title, citations page)	20%		
Process (prewriting, drafts, editing)	20%		
Ideas (narrow topic, 1 idea/paragraph, facts, citations)	20%		
Language (no banned words, clichés, wordiness)	20%		
Grammar/Spelling (punctuation, tenses, sentences, _____)	20%		
TOTAL			

Name _____ Date _____

Passion Pursuit

1. **Brainstorm:** Think of five interests that you have. These could be about anything.

2. **Topic:** Choose one from the list above and circle it.

3. **Explore:** On a separate sheet, create a web of ideas or questions about the topic. Put your topic in the center, and draw lines radiating from it. Fill in facts you know and questions you have.

4. **Narrow:** Look at your web. Where is an area that you'd like to know more about? Circle that branch on the web. This will be your main focus.

5. **Reword:** Write your narrowed focus here. It should include your original topic of interest, but it should be about only one small aspect of it. Have this approved by your teacher.

Focus: _____

6. **Question:** Think of some research questions about your focus. What do you want to learn?

    1.

    2.

    3.

7. **Research:** Gather information that will answer the questions above. As you read, you may feel the need to change your questions or add questions; this is normal. Save or print any articles that may help you, and highlight the information you want to use from each article.

8. **Plan:** Group ideas that should go together. Decide what order the ideas should be in. On another sheet, write an outline or list.

9. **Write:** Start a draft. Be sure not to plagiarize words OR ideas; you must cite all quotations and paraphrasing. Cite as you write. Stick to the facts—your purpose is *to inform*.

10. **Revise:** When you have a draft, consult your notes about introductions and conclusions, and try a technique for each. Create a page for your citations. Think of an engaging title.

Name _____ Date _____

Ponder the Progress

☐ 1. You will write a reflection paper about your progress in class so far this year. (There are no "right" answers to this! Be honest and genuine with yourself.) Complete the **Prewriting Sheet: Ponder the Progress**.

☐ 2. Using your answers from the Prewriting Sheet, write up your reflection. Create paragraphs that seem logical to you. Follow the order of the sheet.

   • A strong **intro** could start with the scene (and sensory details) from #1–2.

   • A strong **conclusion** would be about your dreams and the three ways you could improve in class.

☐ 3. Read what you have. Revise. Think of a title for the piece.

☐ 4. Edit your work. The piece should be at least _____ page(s).

☐ 5. Submit your prewriting, drafts, final copy, and this sheet.

- -

		Preliminary Grade	Revised Grade
Structure (length, paragraphs, title)	20%		
Process (prewriting, editing, drafts)	20%		
Ideas (honest reflection, sensory details)	20%		
Language (no banned words, clichés, wordiness)	20%		
Grammar/Spelling (punctuation, tenses, sentences, _____)	20%		
TOTAL			

Name _____ Date _____

Ponder the Progress

Reflect on your progress so far this year. Answer the following questions on a separate sheet of paper.

1. Describe your best/most fun/proudest moment in this class so far. Use at least **five sensory details.**

2. What did you like about the above moment? What does that tell you about yourself as a learner?

3. What is the most challenging part of this class for you? Why is that?

4. How have you tried your best in this class? What assignments, activities, or habits do you work the hardest on in here? List three.

5. What do you let slide? Why, do you think?

6. Have you participated (in class and out of class) to the best of your ability? List three ways you participate well and three ways you could improve your participation.

7. What is holding you back from participating more?

8. What do you think about yourself as a reader, writer, and thinker? Why do you think these things? And what is your proof (events, accomplishments, failures, etc.)?

My Role	Strengths/Weaknesses/Preferences	Why I Think This
Reader		
Writer		
Thinker		

9. Choose one limiting belief from the chart above. What would it say if the opposite were true?

10. What do you want to do in the future—what is your greatest dream, even if it's just a hunch right now?

11. Come up with **three ways** that this class connects to your dream or vision, even if you feel like you're stretching it a bit!

12. List **three specific ways** you can push yourself to improve as the year goes on.

Persuasive Writing

Strong persuasive writing requires the skills of both effective narrative and expository writing, with the ability to put forth and defend one's own ideas. This section includes a mix of opinion, persuasive, and argumentative pieces to fully explore the genre. Note that at the end of this section, I have included several analyses and given them an argumentative slant. These incorporate the skills students will need throughout high school and beyond. The Writing Assignments and Prewriting Sheets start on page 94, and the writing models are online; see page 127. The standards for persuasive writing are shown at right.

35 Travel Brochure

For travel brochures, the claim essentially is "You should come to _____ because _____." The wording and reasons will vary, but the main idea will not: "Visit here." This claim can be easily supported with facts, like the populations or attractions. Thus, students can clearly examine the difference between fact and opinion. In addition, they can see that although a fact cannot operate as a claim, facts can instead be used to back a thesis in a persuasive way. Students can write about

MULTIMEDIA IDEA

The brochure can be made on paper or as a video or slide show.

MAIN STANDARD

Write opinion, persuasive, and argumentative pieces to support claims on a variety of topics or within analyses, using sound reasoning and enough pertinent evidence.

ADDITIONAL STANDARDS

▶ Generate cohesive pieces focusing on the assignment, purpose, and audience.

▶ Participate in the writing process (reading, prewriting, drafting, revising, and editing).

▶ Demonstrate a clear understanding of the conventions of English.

▶ Demonstrate an ability to use effective figurative language and appropriate vocabulary depending on assignment, purpose, and audience.

a well-known place, or a lesser-known place, using research. As with other activities, all research should be cited. For Part 2 of the assignment, students can transform their information into physical brochures, videos, or slide shows (like Prezi, PowerPoint, or Powtoon). You may need to give extra instruction and guidance on those. Note that the rubric has been slightly altered to allow grading for visual content. The model writing is available online as Resource 35.3; see page 127 for instructions on how to access.

36 Product Review

For this activity, you could either copy "Most Helpful" and "Least Helpful" reviews or let students browse around and find their own. Sites like Amazon, Best Buy, and Target will probably have the most reviews, but students will be motivated to find reviews of products on sites that interest them most. (Keep in mind, a "product" can be a physical object or something intangible, like a video game or app.) Explain to students that their claim is their opinion, and it may come at the beginning of the review, the end, or both. Either way, the reasons in the review should support the claim. This activity also lends itself to a discussion about purpose and audience. One important note: A "Helpful" review is not necessarily perfectly or deeply written—use this fact as a talking point about purpose and audience. In addition, you can have a whole class discussion about the elements of a "Most Helpful" review. (And post a summary of the discussion in the classroom so students can see it as they write.) Be sure to emphasize that negative reviews can be helpful. When finished, students can post their reviews online, if permitted by their parents.

> **MULTIMEDIA IDEA**
> Students can include a picture, video, or chart to enhance their review. Or, the final "draft" of this assignment could be a longer video.

37 Book Review

Like the Product Review, a Book Review's claim is the writer's opinion of the book, and it can appear at the beginning and/or end of the review. Students should examine several "Most" and "Least" helpful book reviews from Amazon or Goodreads. I like to give at least one photocopied review to the entire class for discussion, and I choose books I know they have all read. From this discussion, we create a chart of helpful characteristics to hang in the classroom. Review with students the common use of the term "SPOILER ALERT!" and discuss an awareness of audience for this piece. Although a summary and understanding of literary elements is important when writing a book review, students must also have an opinion—for many, this may seem intimidating, as they rarely know how to go beyond a thought like "It was good" or "I didn't like it." The "How to Have an Opinion about Literature" sheet should help. Emphasize to students that the Prewriting Sheet is there to help them generate ideas only; they shouldn't write to mimic the questions. When finished, students can post their reviews to Amazon or Goodreads. How to Have an Opinion About Literature is available online as Resource 37.3; see page 127 for instructions on how to access.

38 Arts Review

For models, find reviews from a newspaper, magazine, or online of newly released movies, albums, plays, or concerts; you could also search for a certain movie that you know most students have seen. Like the Book Review, a strong Arts Review summarizes the work while giving opinions; additionally, any spoilers should be indicated. If possible, students can upload their reviews to an appropriate site, if available. How to Have an Opinion About the Arts is available online as Resource 38.3; see page 127 for instructions on how to access.

39 Parental Persuasion

This essay is always an entertaining one to read! If the students have not been introduced to the concepts of logos, pathos, and ethos, you might want to spend some time there. I like to do a lesson where the class examines print ads and commercials for examples of the concepts. When students write the essay and highlight the parts they think contain logos, pathos, or ethos, you will know for sure if they understood or not. A fun extension would be to have students record the essay as a speech. You could even have parents respond! The model writing is available online as Resource 39.3; see page 127 for instructions on how to access.

MULTIMEDIA IDEA
Record the essay as a speech, and let students use props or pop-ups.

40 Letter to the Principal

This assignment lets students address an issue they see at school, whether it be large or small. Students should practice using a letter format, unless you want to send the letters as emails, in which case the addresses and date could be omitted. This piece also asks students to consider the "other side's" view on the issue, an important skill in effective persuasion and argumentation. The Idea Sheet: Letter to the Principal and model writing are available online as Resources 40.3 and 40.4; see page 127 for instructions on how to access.

41 Letter for Social Change

Students will broaden their sights for this assignment, choosing issues that are larger than home and school (as in Activities 39 and 40). They will most likely need help finding the appropriate audience. Depending on the recipient, the audience could be a public servant, corporation, small business owner, celebrity figure—anyone who has power to address the topic. You should plan on having students send these, and they will definitely need help addressing the envelopes. They may even receive a letter in return. This assignment reinforces the skills of crafting and supporting a claim as well as persuading an actual audience, and is also an opportunity to emphasize paragraph order. The model writing is available online as Resource 41.3; see page 127 for instructions on how to access.

42 Public Service Announcement

This script and video is best done in groups; students could even use their topics from the Letter for Social Change, if applicable. Find public service announcements online (several can be found on adcouncil.org and by searching the term "public service announcement" on YouTube); students can watch them individually or as a whole class. Help students understand how visual and auditory input can be persuasive. This is a good chance to emphasize the persuasive nature of the piece—that the goal is to get viewers to act. In addition, you could highlight the concept of audience and different audiences.

POST IT

When finished, these Public Service Announcement videos can be posted to the school or class site.

43 Personal Essay

Francis Bacon carried a notebook with him with topic headings such as "Love" and "Trust" on the tops of each page; when he encountered a quotation or new idea about a topic, he jotted it on the appropriate page. Eventually, the notebook became the basis for his most famous work, *The Essays*. Students will do something similar here, choosing a topic, taking a stance about it, and defending their claim with bits of autobiography, allusion, and research. The model writing is available online as Resource 43.3; see page 127 for instructions on how to access.

FUN FACT

Analysis literally means "to loosen"— I like to tell students that when we analyze something, we loosen up the finished product so we can examine and interpret the parts.

44 Analysis of a Song

This is the first activity in a series of "analyses" assignments. Help students understand that analyses are ultimately argumentative; the writer's interpretation of a song, poem, painting, character, short story, or article is essentially a well-crafted opinion supported with evidence from the piece. As students head into the upper grades and beyond, this skill—defending one's careful interpretation—will become ever more relevant. A song is an appropriate place to start: Many people, based on tastes, will disagree about the effectiveness of any given song. It is important to show students that through attentive analysis, one's overall impression, interpretation, or opinion can be intelligently defended. Remind students to use songs that are suitable for school—most songs have "clean" versions if needed. On the Prewriting Sheet, students are instructed to print the lyrics to their songs, so they can annotate them. Students may need help understanding how repetition, pace, and instruments can contribute to the overall meaning of a song; it would help to analyze a song as a whole class to demonstrate how the smaller parts of a song add up to create an overall product. For a whole-class model, choose an oldie like Louis Armstrong's "What a Wonderful World" or John Lennon's "Imagine"—something students are not likely to use for their own papers. Help students correctly cite any quoted lyrics, and finally, remind students to mention the song title and the artist in the introduction. The model writing is available online as Resource 44.3; see page 127 for instructions on how to access.

REMINDER

In all analyses, students should mention the author and title of the work in the introduction. Help students format different types of titles.

45 Analysis of a Poem

The model essays are included here, but you must compile your own packet of poems. The poems on my suggested list are poems accessible to the junior high grades; additionally, you can use poems that are in your curriculum already or that relate to your readings. Of course, students can find their own poems, but I've found that they often can't find accessible poems from reliable sites and resort to random internet poetry that lacks craft and depth. Several high-quality anthologies exist for this age group; my favorites include *Poetry 180* by Billy Collins (2003) and *Poetry Speaks Who I Am* by Elise Paschen (2010). You may have to work with each student to help find poems he or she both understands and is interested in. The model pieces, analyses of "We Real Cool" by Gwendolyn Brooks and "Woman With Flower" by Naomi Long Madgett, are available online as Resource 45.3; see page 127 for instructions on how to access.

46 Analysis of Art

Analyzing art might be new to many students; you might want to walk students through a model as a whole-class exercise. Begin by having students examine a painting and ask repeatedly what they notice—the longer they look, the more they will notice—and then begin to nudge them toward questions about the artist's purpose. Eventually try to arrive at some possible interpretations of the painting's deeper meanings. This can be done with as many paintings as you wish; if you have artwork related to any of the class's readings, even better. I have found that having students view artwork on tablets or even phones can be helpful, since they have the ability to zoom in on details that might not be visible on a classroom screen. As with the Analysis of a Poem, students may need help finding a painting to write about; you may want to provide titles as choices, or have the whole class individually analyze the same painting. Wonderful whole-class examples include Hokusia's *The Great Wave Off Kanagawa* (1830), Bruegel's *Landscape with the Fall of Icarus* (1590), and De Almeida's *La Familia* (2010). The model writing, an analysis of *The Great Wave Off Kanagawa*, is available online as Resource 46.3; see page 127 for instructions on how to access.

CROSS-CURRICULAR OPPORTUNITY
You may want to reach out to your school's art teacher for more guidance or to create a cross-curricular activity for the Analysis of Art activity.

BONUS STANDARD
The Analysis of Art activity also fulfills the standard of interpreting visual content based on evidence, thereby cultivating visual literacy.

47 Analysis of a Character

Verbalizing and defending a character's traits is an accessible form of literary analysis—students are taught in elementary grade lit circles to do this. You may need to give students extra guidance with citing quotes; be sure to have them mention the title and author of the story in their introduction. To give this activity depth, I like to steer students toward finding mixed, or even contradictory, traits within the same character. The model writing is available online as Resource 47.3; see page 127 for instructions on how to access.

48 Analysis of a Short Story

The model essay here is about Richard Connell's "The Most Dangerous Game." Students can understand the essay without reading the story, but if possible, give students an example using a story they've read, or have them read "The Most Dangerous Game" before reading the analysis. The model writing is available online as Resource 48.3; see page 127 for instructions on how to access.

49 Analysis of an Article

This activity can be tricky because students are writing a piece of nonfiction analyzing another piece of nonfiction; they are writing a claim about an author's use of a claim. However, analyzing and evaluating argumentative writing is an essential skill for senior high, college, and beyond. For this assignment, the most effective model would be an analysis of a current op-ed piece; this will require creating one yourself from a current source. Have students read the original article and the analysis—it might help to have students read the sample article in partners or groups, formulate a group consensus about the effectiveness of the article, and then read the analysis. As with the other activities before this, you could have students find their own articles to evaluate, give them a smaller selection from which to choose, or assign one article to the entire class.

50 Connection Inspection

Making a case for meaningful connections is a high-level skill. Students will need help finding ways to connect works that go beyond surface comparisons. The good news is that they enjoy doing it, especially if they can use their own favorite shows, movies, or songs. You may want to specify one of the connections; that is, you can assign that at least one work be about a reading from class. From there, you will probably need to help students find topics; do this by questioning them about what interests them in the class reading. Other students may have two works they want to connect, but they will need help going deeper into the works. One way to see more complexity is to use an "Although" or "Even though" structure in the claim, focusing on some similarities, but also a difference or two. In addition, the prewriting chart may not exactly fit all topics; help students organize their ideas logically. As always, ideas reveal themselves in the writing process, so let students start and see what comes up. You could have students work on some preliminary ideas (#1–3 on the Prewriting Sheet) and then meet in pairs to discuss how to go further with their topics. The model writing is available online as Resource 50.3; see page 127 for instructions on how to access.

Name _____ Date _____

Travel Brochure

Part 1: Research and Write

☐ 1. Read the sample essay. Answer the questions given.

☐ 2. Think of a place you have lived in or visited. It should be a place you think other people should see. Complete the **Prewriting Sheet: Travel Brochure**.

☐ 3. Write out a draft of the brochure as a regular document for now, completing #7–10 on the Prewriting Sheet.

☐ 4. Read your draft and make changes on it. Be sure that you have the following:

_____ an interesting introduction

_____ each reason in its own paragraph

_____ in each reason paragraph, other examples and details about that reason

_____ an interesting conclusion

_____ a citation page, citing your sources

☐ 5. Edit your draft. Your paper should be at least _____ page(s). Write a title.

Part 2: Design and Present

☐ 6. Transform the information into a visual format. Choose one of the following:

- Copy and paste your writing into a brochure program, adding pictures.
- Use your writing to create a script for a video. Film the video.

☐ 7. Submit your brochure in its visual form and written form, with your prewriting, drafts, and this sheet.

		Preliminary Grade	Revised Grade
Structure (length, paragraphs, citation page, title, visual form)	20%		
Process (prewriting, drafts, editing)	20%		
Ideas (claim, reasons, research, intro, conclusion; no banned words, clichés, or wordiness)	20%		
Visual (engaging and apt visuals; persuasive)	20%		
Grammar/Spelling (punctuation, tenses, sentences, _____)	20%		
TOTAL			

Name _____ Date _____

Travel Brochure

1. **Topic:** What place will you write about?

2. **Brainstorm:** What do you know about this place? On a separate sheet, brainstorm your ideas as a list or mind map. Think of your five senses, as well as any other information that makes this place interesting or enjoyable.

3. **Claim:** For a preliminary claim, finish this sentence with the name of your place:

   Visit _____ .

4. **Research:** Conduct some research on your topic. When you find information that supports your claim (why your place is interesting or enjoyable), save or bookmark the articles, and highlight the relevant information. In addition, look for some basic information about the place (location, size, etc.) that could be used in the introduction. Be sure to note all source information (author, website, date).

5. **Organize:** Looking at your brainstorm and at your research, form two to four groups of main ideas about why someone should visit your place. The groups should support your claim.

6. **Expand the Claim:** Using the main ideas from your "reason" groups (#5), add to your claim (#3). Try to introduce each group with just a word or phrase. Write yours below:

7. **Draft:** Write up the claim and reason paragraphs in a regular document for now. If you need to add details to any of your paragraphs, conduct more research.

8. **Conclusion:** Look at your conclusion techniques. What could work here?

9. **Introduction:** Choose an introductory technique. Questioning, using sensory details, or using "Imagine . . ." could work especially well in a travel brochure.

10. **Add Visuals:** Find pictures, charts, or videos online that could be used in your travel brochure. Save or bookmark them, and note their sources.

Name _____ Date _____

Product Review

☐ 1. Read at least five "Most Helpful" product reviews and at least five "Least Helpful" product reviews online. Answer the following:

- Find four qualities that make a review "Most Helpful."

- Find three qualities that make a review "Least Helpful."

- What kinds of titles do the "Most Helpful" reviews have? Are they engaging or informational?

- What other elements (photos, videos, charts, lists) appear in the "Most Helpful" reviews?

- What are the introductory techniques in the "Most Helpful" reviews? What are the conclusion techniques?

☐ 2. Complete the **Prewriting Sheet: Product Review**.

☐ 3. Write your review. Be sure to have one main idea per paragraph. The piece should be at least _____ page(s).

☐ 4. Read what you have. Revise. Underline the sentence that contains your claim.

☐ 5. Edit your draft. Upgrade four verbs. Be sure to have a title.

☐ 6. If you are including any visuals, create and save them.

☐ 7. Submit your prewriting, drafts, final copy, and this sheet.

☐ 8. When ready, upload your review to the appropriate site.

		Preliminary Grade	Revised Grade
Structure (length, paragraphs, title)	20%		
Process (prewriting, editing, drafts)	20%		
Ideas (opinion, reasons, conclusion, intro)	20%		
Language (no banned words, clichés, wordiness)	20%		
Grammar/Spelling (punctuation, tenses, sentences, _____)	20%		
TOTAL			

Name _____ Date _____

Product Review

1. **Topic:** What is the product you will review? Be sure it is something you know well and have used many times. Give a brief description of it, using the back if necessary.

2. **Qualities:** What are the positives and negatives about this product? Use sensory details.

Positives		Negatives	
Quality	Details	Quality	Details

3. **Conclusion:** What is your overall conclusion about this product? How many stars?

4. **Introduction:** What would be an interesting way to begin this review?

5. **Title:** What is an engaging title for this review?

6. **Visuals:** What are some visuals you could add (photos, videos, charts, and so on)? Be specific.

Name _____   Date _____

Book Review

☐ 1. Read at least five "Most Helpful" book reviews and at least five "Least Helpful" book reviews online. Answer the following:

- Find four qualities that make a review "Most Helpful."
- Find three qualities that make a review "Least Helpful."
- What kinds of titles do the "Most Helpful" reviews have? Are they engaging or informational?
- What are the introductory techniques in the "Most Helpful" reviews? What are the conclusion techniques?

☐ 2. Complete the **Prewriting Sheet: Book Review**, including **How to Have an Opinion About Literature**.

☐ 3. On another sheet, brainstorm some possible paragraphs around your main ideas. Formulate your ideas into a cohesive review—you don't have to write in the order of the Prewriting Sheet. Weave together your opinions with evidence and quotations from the book.

☐ 4. Write your review. Be sure to have one main idea per paragraph. The piece should be at least _____ page(s). **If you are including a spoiler, be sure to indicate that for your readers by prefacing the section with "SPOILER ALERT!"**

☐ 5. Read what you have. Revise. Underline the sentence that contains your claim.

☐ 6. Edit your draft. Upgrade four verbs. Be sure you have a title.

☐ 7. Submit your prewriting, drafts, final copy, and this sheet.

☐ 8. When ready, upload your review to the appropriate site.

		Preliminary Grade	Revised Grade
Structure (length, paragraphs, title)	20%		
Process (prewriting, editing, drafts)	20%		
Ideas (opinion, reasons, conclusion, intro)	20%		
Language (no banned words, clichés, wordiness)	20%		
Grammar/Spelling (punctuation, tenses, sentences, _____)	20%		
TOTAL			

Name _____ Date _____

Book Review

1. Title of book: _____ Author: _____

2. Give a BRIEF Summary:

3. List the main character(s): 1. _____

   2. _____

4. What was the biggest struggle for the main character?

5. How was this struggle finally resolved?

6. How did this character change during the story?

7. Looking at your answer to the previous question, what is the theme or message of this story?

8. How would you describe the author's writing style? (Think about vocabulary, sentence length, descriptions, the tone of voice of the narrator, and the overall mood of the book.)

9. Give one or two quotations (with pages) from the book that support any of your answers above.

10. Now, complete the **How to Have an Opinion About Literature** sheet.

Name _____   Date _____

Arts Review

☐   1. Read the model review. Answer the following:

- Is this a positive, negative, or mixed review? What are the reasons?
- How does the review begin?
- How does it end?
- Describe the writer's tone and find examples to support your ideas.

☐   2. Complete the **Prewriting Sheet: Arts Review**, including **How to Have an Opinion About the Arts**.

☐   3. Write your review. Be sure to have one main idea per paragraph. The piece should be at least _____ page(s). **If you are including a spoiler, be sure to indicate that for your readers by prefacing the section with "SPOILER ALERT!"**

☐   4. Read what you have. Revise. Underline the sentence that contains your claim.

☐   5. Edit your draft. Upgrade four verbs. Think of a title.

☐   6. Submit your prewriting, drafts, final copy, and this sheet.

☐   7. When ready, upload your review to the appropriate site.

		Preliminary Grade	Revised Grade
Structure (length, paragraphs, title)	20%		
Process (prewriting, editing, drafts)	20%		
Ideas (opinion, reasons, conclusion, intro)	20%		
Language (no banned words, clichés, wordiness)	20%		
Grammar/Spelling (punctuation, tenses, sentences, _____)	20%		
TOTAL			

50 Writing Activities for Meeting Higher Standards © Marilyn Pryle • Scholastic Inc.

Name _____ Date _____

Arts Review

1. Choose a movie, album, play, or concert to review. Write the title and artist here:

2. What are your initial thoughts about this piece? On a separate sheet, brainstorm
    any ideas.

3. Complete the appropriate section on the **How to Have an Opinion About the Arts** sheet.

4. Look at your ideas. Will this be a positive, negative, or mixed review?

5. Group your ideas into possible paragraphs. Make sure each paragraph has only one main idea.
    On your paper, **label the main idea** for each paragraph-group.

6. Look at your groups. Is there anywhere you could add a quotation from the piece? Verify the
    quotation and cite it.

7. What would be an interesting way to start this review? Try something below:

8. What could you write about for a conclusion?

9. Think of a possible title or two. Make it clever—don't simply repeat the title of the piece.

10. Is there a visual you could include? What would it be, and where would you find it?

Name _____ Date _____

Parental Persuasion

1. Read the model and answer the following:
   - What action does the writer want his parents to take?
   - What does the writer use as logical reasoning to support his claim?
   - What does the writer do for an emotional appeal?
   - What does the writer say to prove he is worthy of the action?
   - Categorize the introductory and conclusion techniques.

2. Complete the **Prewriting Sheet: Parental Persuasion**.

3. Write your draft. On the top, label the **audience** and **purpose** for this piece.

4. Read what you have. Revise. Underline the sentence that contains your **claim**.

5. Edit your draft. Upgrade four verbs.

6. Use different colored highlighters to **label** your logos, pathos, and ethos.

7. Submit your prewriting, drafts, final copy, and this sheet.

EXTRA: Record your essay as a speech, using your voice and gestures to emphasize the logos, pathos, and ethos. Upload to the assigned space.

		Preliminary Grade	Revised Grade
Structure (length, paragraphs)	20%		
Process (prewriting, editing, drafts)	20%		
Ideas (claim, logos, pathos, ethos, conclusion, intro, purpose & audience labeled)	20%		
Language (no banned words, clichés, wordiness)	20%		
Grammar/Spelling (punctuation, tenses, sentences, _____)	20%		
TOTAL			

Name _____ Date _____

Parental Persuasion

1. Below, brainstorm some possible **issues** that you would like to persuade your parent(s) or guardian(s) about. These can be major or minor:

2. Circle one above. Now, brainstorm some **reasons** for your cause:

3. Persuasion usually draws from three types of arguments: reasoning (logos), emotional appeal (pathos), and trust in the speaker (ethos). Rewrite your reasons in these categories and add to each. Continue on another sheet.

    *   Logos (facts, reasons, numbers, statistics, events):

    *   Pathos (emotional appeal—What would make them feel sad, guilty, or afraid? What would make them laugh or feel joy?)

    *   Ethos (trust in you as a person, your good character)

4. How could you organize this piece? On a separate sheet, group up your ideas into paragraphs.

5. Now, think about how to begin your piece. You could begin with "Imagine . . ." and describe a scene, using pathos. You could begin with a statistic (logos). You could begin by writing about your own character and integrity (ethos). Write down an idea or two below:

6. How could you end this piece? A strong conclusion could also include logos, pathos, or ethos. You could also try an *if/then* sentence. What reason might make a powerful ending?

Name _____ Date _____

Letter to the Principal

☐ 1. Read the model letter and answer the questions given.

☐ 2. Complete the **Idea Sheet: Letter to the Principal**.

☐ 3. Complete the **Prewriting Sheet: Letter to the Principal**.

☐ 4. Write a draft of your letter. Be sure to have one main idea per paragraph and details for each. #4 and #5 on the Prewriting Sheet should be combined into one paragraph.

☐ 5. Use a letter format. Your letter should be at least _____ page(s).

☐ 6. Read what you have. Revise. Underline the sentence that contains your claim.

☐ 7. Try at least two or more transition words, such as:

   • *plus, in addition, moreover, also*   • *however, on the other hand*

   • *first, second, third, finally*   • *therefore, hence, as a result*

☐ 8. Reread your draft and revise again. Upgrade four verbs. Edit your work.

☐ 9. Submit your prewriting, drafts, final copy, and this sheet.

- -

		Preliminary Grade	Revised Grade
Structure (letter format, paragraphs, length)	20%		
Process (prewriting, editing, drafts)	20%		
Ideas (claim, 1 main idea per paragraph, details, intro, conclusion)	20%		
Language (no banned words, clichés, wordiness; strong verbs, transition words)	20%		
Grammar/Spelling (punctuation, tenses, sentences, _____)	20%		
TOTAL			

50 Writing Activities for Meeting Higher Standards © Marilyn Pryle • Scholastic Inc

Name _____ Date _____

Letter to the Principal

1. Look at your list from the Idea Sheet. Choose one issue to use as your topic. Write your thoughts as a full sentence below. (You could try using the word *should*.)

2. That sentence will be your **claim**. Now, brainstorm any ideas about it that you may have. Jot down any **reasons**, **examples**, **images**, or **feelings** you can think of.

3. Looking at your brainstorm, group your ideas together on another sheet. You might add or subtract ideas as you do. Remember the persuasive techniques of logos, pathos, and ethos.

4. What if someone disagreed with you? What would that person say? Add to your sheet.

5. What would you say back to that person? Why is that person wrong?

6. Is there a solution to your problem? What would it be? What would the principal have to do?

7. Try an *if/then* sentence to use as your clincher. Start with "If you . . ."

8. What is an attention-getting way to begin? Can you create a scenario, use a statistic, or ask an engaging question? Should you start by establishing your own integrity? Jot down some ideas.

Name _____ Date _____

Letter for Social Change

☐ 1. Read the sample letter and answer the following questions:

- What technique is used for the introduction? What is the claim?
- In your opinion, what is the author's strongest reason?
- What is the other side's view?
- What technique is used for the conclusion?
- Circle three transition words, three strong verbs, and three sensory details.

☐ 2. Think of an issue you want to write about. Complete the **Prewriting Sheet: Letter for Social Change**.

☐ 3. Write a rough draft, using a letter format. Have one main idea per paragraph.

☐ 4. Read the letter. Revise. Make sure you have the following:

____ an attention-grabbing introduction   ____ supporting evidence for each reason

____ examples and sensory details   ____ the other side's view

____ transition words   ____ a strong conclusion

____ closing and signature   ____ your address, recipient's address, date

☐ 5. Reread your draft and revise again. Upgrade four verbs. Edit your work. Your letter should be _____ page(s).

☐ 6. Submit your prewriting, drafts, final copy, and this sheet.

- -

		Preliminary Grade	Revised Grade
Structure (letter format, paragraphs, length)	20%		
Process (prewriting, editing, drafts)	20%		
Ideas (claim, 1 main idea per paragraph, details, intro, conclusion)	20%		
Language (no banned words, clichés, wordiness; strong verbs, transition words)	20%		
Grammar/Spelling (punctuation, tenses, sentences, _____)	20%		
TOTAL			

    50 Writing Activities for Meeting Higher Standards © Marilyn Pryle • Scholastic Inc

Name _____ Date _____

Letter for Social Change

1. On another sheet of paper, brainstorm some social issues you feel strongly about.
    These can be large or small.

2. Choose one issue from your list and circle it. Who would be the appropriate audience for a
    letter urging change about it? Think of government officials (mayor, representative, senator,
    president), other leaders, and businesses. Write down a possible recipient.

3. Write your feelings on the issue as a full sentence. This will be your claim.

4. Brainstorm any ideas about your issue that you may have. Jot down any **reasons, examples,
    images,** or **feelings** you can think of. Think about the techniques of logos, pathos, and ethos.
    Use the internet to research additional reasons, and cite your sources.

5. Looking at your brainstorm, group your ideas together. You might add or subtract ideas as
    you do.

6. What if someone disagreed with you? What would that person say? Add to your sheet.

7. What would you say back to that person? Why is that person wrong? (#6 and #7 should be
    written about in a paragraph.)

8. Look at your paragraph-groups. What would be the best order for them in the letter? Put your
    strongest reason last. Number the groups in the order you want them to appear.

9. Is there a solution to your problem? What would it be? What would the recipient have to do?
    Usually, the solution or call to action makes a strong conclusion.

10. Try an *if/then* sentence as a possible clincher. Start with "If you . . ."

11. What is an attention-getting way to begin? Can you create a scenario, use a statistic, or ask an
    engaging question? Should you start by establishing your own integrity? Jot down some ideas.

12. Research the recipient's address and use it for your letter and envelope.

Name _____ Date _____

Public Service Announcement

☐ 1. View several public service announcements and answer the following questions:

- What is the message (or claim) of the announcement?

- Who is the target audience?

- What are the supporting reasons? List them all, and then label them as factual (logos), emotional (pathos), or trusting the messenger (ethos).

- How does the visual and auditory nature of the message enhance the content?

☐ 2. Complete the **Prewriting Sheet: Public Service Announcement**.

☐ 3. Record your PSA. It should be at least _____ but no longer than _____ minutes.

☐ 4. Review and edit your PSA. Be sure that:

- Your beginning attracts viewers' attention

- You use engaging visuals and sound

- Your message is clear

- You use logos, pathos, and ethos

- Viewers know what to do by the end

☐ 5. Upload your video to the assigned spot.

		Preliminary Grade	Revised Grade
Structure (video, length, title)	20%		
Process (prewriting, filming)	20%		
Ideas (claim, logos, pathos, ethos, call to action)	20%		
Audio/Visual (quality of visuals and sounds, appropriate language, pacing, order)	20%		
Grammar/Spelling (punctuation, tenses, sentences, _____)	20%		
TOTAL			

50 Writing Activities for Meeting Higher Standards © Marilyn Pryle • Scholastic Inc.

Name _____ Date _____

Public Service Announcement

1. On another sheet of paper, brainstorm some topics you care about that could become a public service announcement.

2. Choose one and circle it. Write out the message you want to communicate with your PSA. **Note your target audience.**

3. Next, brainstorm any reasons that would support the message.

4. Add to your reasons with research (statistics, facts, examples, dates, etc.). Be sure to cite all sources.

5. Look at all of your reasons. Label them as one of the three categories below. If you are missing one of the categories, add reasoning in that category. Remember that your reasoning can be visual and auditory, since this will be a video.

    ☐ Logos—facts, statistics, events, dates, percentages

    ☐ Pathos—Any image or thought that causes the viewer to feel an emotion, positive or negative (joy, hope, sadness, fear, anger, and so on). Remember that colors can cause emotional responses.

    ☐ Ethos—Anything that establishes the trustworthiness of the speaker (in this case, you).

6. On another sheet, plan your PSA. Arrange your reasons and message in the most effective order. Here are some questions to consider:

    ☐ What is a powerful way to begin, to get viewers' attention? What visual and auditory input can you use?

    ☐ In what order should you present your reasons? What order is most effective?

    ☐ Can you use text in the PSA?

    ☐ Will you use people acting, or visual images, or both?

    ☐ Will viewers know what action to take by the end of the PSA?

7. When ready, record your PSA.

Name _____ Date _____

Personal Essay

☐ 1. Read the model essay. Answer the following questions:
- What is the author's claim about the topic?
- What technique does the author use for an introduction?
- How does the author draw from personal experience?
- What other examples does the author use?
- What technique is employed for the conclusion?

☐ 2. Choose a topic for your own personal essay. Some examples are below, but you can choose anything that is appropriate for school. Look at your Life List for additional help.

Some topics:	Truth	Envy	Gossip	Dating	Bravery
	Fashion	Happiness	Sadness	Parents	Beauty
	Youth	Nature	Writing	History	Lying
	Sports	Solitude	Conscience	Loss	Popularity

☐ 3. Complete the **Prewriting Sheet: Personal Essay.**

☐ 4. Write a first draft. It should be at least _____ page(s).

☐ 5. Revise the draft and edit your work. Check for:

_____ a title: "On . . ."   _____ a quotation

_____ an attention-grabbing introduction   _____ transition words

_____ a true story   _____ strong verbs (change at least three)

_____ an additional supporting work   _____ a strong conclusion

☐ 6. Submit your prewriting, drafts, final copy, and this sheet.

· ·

		Preliminary Grade	Revised Grade
Structure (length, paragraphs, title)	20%		
Process (prewriting, editing, drafts)	20%		
Ideas (claim, intro, conclusion, true story, supporting work, quotation)	20%		
Language (no banned words, clichés, wordiness; sentence variation, transition words)	20%		
Grammar/Spelling (punctuation, tenses, sentences, _____)	20%		
TOTAL			

50 Writing Activities for Meeting Higher Standards © Marilyn Pryle • Scholastic Inc.

Name _____ Date _____

Personal Essay

1. What topic will your essay be about?

2. Write down a definition of your topic (either your own or from the dictionary):

3. Write down your personal feelings or opinion about your topic. Is it good? bad? useful? important? easy? difficult? common? rare? What do you want to say about it? **Brainstorm** some ideas:

4. Think of one or two real-life stories that illustrate your topic and your feelings. For example, if you're writing about the dangers of anger, you could tell about a time when you (or someone) got angry and lost a friendship or something else important. This should be a true story from your life.

5. Look up a quote related to your topic. Copy that quote and its author. You can have more than one.

6. Think about other examples that illustrate your topic (from books, short stories, poems, history, movies, etc.). Add at least one and cite it.

7. What's your final conclusion about your topic?

8. What is an interesting way to start this essay? Write a possible first sentence below:

On another sheet of paper, take these ideas and group them in an order that seems right to you.

Name _____ Date _____

Analysis of a Song

☐ 1. Read the model essay and answer the following questions:
- What is the author's overall feeling about the song?
- What proof does the author give to support this feeling?
- How does imagery contribute to the overall meaning of the song?
- How does repetition contribute to the overall meaning?
- How does the music itself reinforce the song's meaning?

☐ 2. Complete the **Prewriting Sheet: Analysis of a Song**.

☐ 3. Look at the information from the other questions on the Prewriting Sheet. Look at your annotations. What specific examples can support your claim and interpretation of the song? Form at least three main ideas, and list them. Beside each main idea, list your specific examples. Use quotes from the song.

☐ 4. Using your plan, write up a draft. Be sure that each paragraph has only one main idea with examples. Cite your quotes. Your analysis should be _____ page(s).

☐ 5. When finished, write an engaging introduction. Your claim should be part of it. Then write a strong conclusion, reiterating your main ideas without outright repeating. Leave the reader with something to think about.

☐ 6. Reread your draft and revise. Upgrade four verbs. Edit your work.

☐ 7. Submit your prewriting, drafts, final copy, and this sheet.

		Preliminary Grade	Revised Grade
Structure (length, paragraphs, title)	20%		
Process (prewriting, drafts, editing)	20%		
Ideas (claim, 1 main idea per paragraph, details, use of quotes, intro, conclusion)	20%		
Language (no banned words, clichés, wordiness; strong verbs, transition words)	20%		
Grammar/Spelling (punctuation, tenses, sentences, _____)	20%		
TOTAL			

Name _____ Date _____

Analysis of a Song

1. Choose a song you would like to analyze. Write the title and artist below:

2. Find lyrics to the song online. If possible, print them so you can annotate. Or, save them to a document that you can annotate on the screen.

3. Read the lyrics. What is this song about? What is the topic? Is there a claim? What is the mood of the song? Write down some initial ideas on a sheet of paper.

4. Annotate the song:

    ☐ Note any imagery in the song. What are the sights and colors, (described) sounds, smells, textures, or tastes? Label them.

    ☐ Circle or highlight any rhyming words.

    ☐ Underline any repetition or parallelism (partial repetition).

    ☐ Note any similes or metaphors.

    ☐ Note any other literary devices, such as onomatopoeia or personification.

5. On your paper, answer these questions: What is the effect of the above techniques? Does the rhyming make the song more upbeat, sad, or wistful? What mood do the similes and metaphors create? How so?

6. Now answer these questions: What parts are repeated the most? What is the effect of this? Do these lines relate to the main idea of the song?

7. Think about the music. Label the parts that are slower or faster, softer or louder. What is the effect of this? Does the variation help communicate the main idea? Write about it on your paper.

8. Are there any particular instruments that stand out in the song? How so? Does it contribute to the song's meaning? Write about it on your paper.

9. Now, tie it all together. What is this song trying to do? What is it trying to express? How is the listener supposed to feel? How do the images, rhyming, repetition, and other devices contribute to this? How does the music contribute to this? Write out your ideas on your paper.

10. Does this song succeed in what it is trying to do? How so, or why not? Craft a claim out of this idea and write it on your paper.

Name _____ Date _____

Analysis of a Poem

☐ 1. Read the two model analyses and their accompanying poems. Answer the questions that go with them.

☐ 2. Choose a poem to analyze. Complete the **Prewriting Sheet: Analysis of a Poem**.

☐ 3. Formulate a claim for your analysis, focusing on the last question of the Prewriting Sheet.

☐ 4. Look at the information from the other questions on the Prewriting Sheet. Look at your annotations. What specific examples can support your claim and interpretation of the poem? Form at least three main ideas, and list them. Beside each main idea, list your specific examples. Use quotes from the poem.

☐ 5. Using your plan, write up a draft. Be sure that each paragraph has only one main idea with examples. Cite your quotes. Your analysis should be _____ page(s).

☐ 6. When finished, try an engaging introduction. Your claim should be part of it. Then try a strong conclusion, reiterating your main ideas without outright repeating. Leave the reader with something to think about.

☐ 7. Reread your draft and revise. Upgrade four verbs. Edit your work.

☐ 8. Submit your prewriting, drafts, final copy, and this sheet.

		Preliminary Grade	Revised Grade
Structure (length, paragraphs, title)	20%		
Process (prewriting, drafts, editing)	20%		
Ideas (claim, 1 main idea per paragraph, details, use of quotes, intro, conclusion)	20%		
Language (no banned words, clichés, wordiness; strong verbs, transition words)	20%		
Grammar/Spelling (punctuation, tenses, sentences, _____)	20%		
TOTAL			

Name _____ Date _____

Analysis of a Poem

Title of Poem: _____ Author: _____

Write your responses on a separate sheet of paper.

Brainstorm: Jot down any thoughts you have about the poem: reactions, ideas, images, anything.

Form of Poem:

How many stanzas? _____ Is it free verse? _____ (If yes, skip the next two questions.)

What is the rhyme scheme? ____ _____ What is the meter? _____

Understanding the Poem:

1. Look up any words you don't know and list them with their definitions.

2. Are there any similes or metaphors? Annotate or list them and explain them.

3. Is there any alliteration? Annotate or list it.

4. Any onomatopoeia? Annotate or list it.

5. Any personification? Any assonance?

6. Is there any word or phrase in the poem that is repeated? List it.

7. Are there any sensory details that jump out at you? Could they be symbols for something else?

Line-by-Line Paraphrase: Write some of the lines on the left, and rewrite them in your own words.

Poem	Your own words

Title: What does the title of the poem mean? Could it have a double meaning? What is it?

Theme: What could be a deeper meaning of the poem?

Form: Does the form of the poem (line length, alliteration, meter, etc.) relate to the theme/topic? (For example, a poem about **silence** might have a **short last line**, to give the feeling of silence. Or a poem about the **wind** might have **alliteration with the letter "s,"** to sound like the wind.)

Claim: What is this poem attempting to do? Does it only describe, or does it make a point? What techniques does it use to achieve the overall effect? Your claim will be the basis for your analysis.

Name _____   Date _____

Analysis of Art

☐ 1. Examine the painting used as a sample for this activity. Answer the following questions:

- What do you notice about this painting? List at least ten ideas.
- What is the mood of this painting? Why do you think so?
- What is the painter's purpose? What is the deeper meaning or truth here?

☐ 2. Read the model essay and answer the following questions:

- What is the writer's claim about the painting?
- What evidence from the painting supports this claim?
- Do you agree with this writer's interpretation of the painting? Give examples about why and/or why not.

☐ 3. Complete the **Prewriting Sheet: Analysis of Art**.

☐ 4. Formulate an interpretation of the painting, using #8 and #9 on the Prewriting Sheet. Write out your claim on a piece of paper.

☐ 5. Look at the information from the other questions on the Prewriting Sheet. Look at your annotations. What specific examples can support your claim and interpretation of the painting? Form at least three main ideas, and list them. Beside each main idea, list your specific examples from the painting.

☐ 6. Using your plan, write up a draft. Be sure that each paragraph has only one main idea with examples. Your analysis should be _____ page(s).

☐ 7. Be sure to have an engaging intro and a thought-provoking conclusion.

☐ 8. Read your draft and revise. Upgrade four words and add a title. Edit your work.

☐ 9. Submit your prewriting, drafts, final copy, and this sheet.

		Preliminary Grade	Revised Grade
Structure (length, paragraphs, title)	20%		
Process (prewriting, drafts, editing)	20%		
Ideas (claim, 1 main idea per paragraph, details, intro, conclusion)	20%		
Language (no banned words, clichés, wordiness; strong verbs, transition words)	20%		
Grammar/Spelling (punctuation, tenses, sentences, _____)	20%		
TOTAL			

Name _____ Date _____

Analysis of Art

1. Title of Painting: _____ Artist: _____

2. When you look at the painting, what is your eye first drawn to?

3. List, or annotate on the painting, **at least ten ideas** (colors, objects, textures, etc.) that you notice.

4. What is a detail in this painting that you don't notice right away, but might be important to the meaning of the painting?

5. What feels like the mood of this painting? Why?

6. What are the main colors in the painting? How do these contribute to the mood?

7. What else in the painting contributes to the mood?

8. What is the artist trying to communicate? What is a deeper message? What truth about life is revealed in this work?

9. Does the artist succeed in communicating this truth? How so, or why not?

Name _____ Date _____

Analysis of a Character

☐ 1. Read the model essay and answer the following questions:

- What is the writer's claim about the character?

- How does the writer make the character seem three-dimensional?

- What proof does the writer give as evidence for the claim?

- What technique does the writer use for an introduction? A conclusion?

☐ 2. Complete the **Prewriting Sheet: Analysis of a Character**.

☐ 3. Using your prewriting, write up a draft. Be sure that each paragraph has only one main idea with examples. Cite your quotes. Your analysis should be _____ page(s).

☐ 4. Be sure to have an engaging intro and a thought-provoking conclusion.

☐ 5. Read your draft and revise. Upgrade four verbs and think of a title. Edit your work.

☐ 6. Submit your prewriting, drafts, final copy, and this sheet.

		Preliminary Grade	Revised Grade
Structure (length, paragraphs, title)	20%		
Process (prewriting, drafts, editing)	20%		
Ideas (claim, 1 main idea per paragraph, details, use of quotes, intro, conclusion)	20%		
Language (no banned words, clichés, wordiness; strong verbs, transition words)	20%		
Grammar/Spelling (punctuation, tenses, sentences, _____)	20%		
TOTAL			

50 Writing Activities for Meeting Higher Standards © Marilyn Pryle • Scholastic

Name _____ Date _____

Analysis of a Character

1. Character name: _____

   Work: _____ Author: _____

2. Brainstorm some ideas about the character and write them on a separate sheet of paper.

3. Think about your character. What are two or three traits that you could argue for? Write them on your paper and circle them.

4. Now, think of a surprising trait, or one that seems to go against the other traits. For example, a character might be loyal to her country but disloyal to her father. Or, a character might be driven to succeed in school, but unmotivated to earn money. Try to think of a way in which the character is more complex than he or she seems on the surface.

5. Find evidence for your traits. On another sheet, create a chart like the one below:

Character Traits	**Evidence** (actions, words, thoughts—use quotations from the story for each trait, and give the page number for each)
1.	
2.	
3.	
(surprising trait) 4.	

6. Craft a sentence that can be your claim. Try a sentence with "Although . . ." or "Even though . . ." in it, so that you can incorporate the surprising trait.

7. What is a technique that might work for an introduction?

8. What could you try for a conclusion? Remember, give the audience a twist to think about.

Name _____ Date _____

Analysis of a Short Story

☐ 1. Read the model essay and answer the following questions:

  • What is the writer's main interpretation about the story?

  • What evidence does the writer use to support his interpretation?

  • How does the writer's use of quotes from the story help prove his points?

  • Do you feel like the writer understands the story well? Why or why not?

☐ 2. Complete the **Prewriting Sheet: Analysis of a Short Story**.

☐ 3. Using your answers to #9 and #10 on the Prewriting Sheet, formulate an overall interpretation of the story. This will be your claim.

☐ 4. Using your prewriting, write up a draft. Remember that your goal is to discuss the important aspects of the story, while supporting your overall interpretation. Be sure that each paragraph has only one main idea with examples.

☐ 5. Cite your quotes. Your analysis should be _____ page(s).

☐ 6. Be sure to have an engaging intro and a thought-provoking conclusion.

☐ 7. Read your draft and revise. Upgrade four verbs and think of a title. Edit your work.

☐ 8. Submit your prewriting, drafts, final copy, and this sheet.

		Preliminary Grade	Revised Grade
Structure (length, paragraphs, title)	20%		
Process (prewriting, drafts, editing)	20%		
Ideas (claim, 1 main idea per paragraph, details, use of quotes, intro, conclusion)	20%		
Language (no banned words, clichés, wordiness; strong verbs, transition words)	20%		
Grammar/Spelling (punctuation, tenses, sentences, _____)	20%		
TOTAL			

Name _____ Date _____

Analysis of a Short Story

Title of story: _____ Author: _____

Answer questions on a separate sheet of paper.

1. **Brainstorm** any ideas about this story that stand out in your mind.

2. **Plot:** Give a BRIEF summary.

3. **Character:** List the main characters and their traits, with examples and quotes from the text.

Main Characters	Character Traits/Examples/Quotes With Citations

4. **Setting(s)** with details: How does the **setting** contribute to the **mood**?

5. What were some of the **conflicts** in the story? Describe a conflict *within the main character*. Give a **quote** to illustrate it.

6. How did the main character change during the story? What does he/she learn?

7. Based on what you wrote for #6, what is the **theme** or message of this story? Go deep; don't simply write, "The theme of this story is survival." Instead, ask yourself, "What more can I explain about the author's view of survival? What does survival mean in this particular story?"

8. **Symbolism:** Look for images in the book that might be symbols for something deeper. Try to make an in-depth interpretation. For example, instead of merely noticing, "The setting has a lot of water in it," try to interpret what the water symbolizes: fear? mystery? death? abundance of life?

9. What did this author try to accomplish with this story? What is the message or truth about life that the author was trying to convey?

10. Do you think the author succeeded in communicating this truth? How so, or why not?

Name _____ Date _____

Analysis of an Article

☐ 1. Read the article and the analysis of the article. Then answer the following questions.

- What is the analysis writer's main interpretation about the article?

- What evidence does the analysis writer use to support this interpretation?

- How does the analysis writer's use of quotes from the article support his or her points?

- Do you feel like the analysis writer understands the article well? Why or why not?

☐ 2. Complete the **Prewriting Sheet: Analysis of an Article**.

☐ 3. Using your answer to #5 on the Prewriting Sheet, formulate an overall interpretation of the article. This will be your claim.

☐ 4. Using your Prewriting Sheet, write up a draft. Remember that your goal is to discuss the important aspects of the article while supporting your overall interpretation. Be sure that each paragraph has only one main idea with examples.

☐ 5. Cite your quotes. Your analysis should be _____ page(s).

☐ 6. Be sure to have an engaging intro and a thought-provoking conclusion.

☐ 7. Read your draft and revise. Upgrade four verbs and add a title. Edit your work.

☐ 8. Submit your prewriting, drafts, final copy, and this sheet.

		Preliminary Grade	Revised Grade
Structure (length, paragraphs, title)	20%		
Process (prewriting, drafts, editing)	20%		
Ideas (claim, 1 main idea per paragraph, details, use of quotes, intro, conclusion)	20%		
Language (no banned words, clichés, wordiness; strong verbs, transition words)	20%		
Grammar/Spelling (punctuation, tenses, sentences, _____)	20%		
TOTAL			

Name _____ Date _____

Analysis of an Article

1. Title of article: _____

   Author: _____ Date: _____

2. Complete:

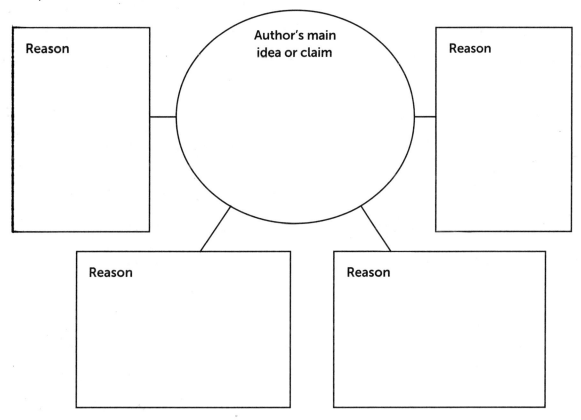

3. What techniques (logos, pathos, ethos, sensory details, figurative language) does the author use to enhance the argument? List them or annotate.

4. Does the author address any opposing views? How so? Was anything omitted?

5. Overall, is the article effective and convincing? Is the claim supported? How so, or why not?

Name _____ Date _____

Connection Inspection

☐ 1. Read the model essay and answer the following questions:

- What claim does the writer make about these two works?

- What examples does the writer give to prove the claim?

- What technique is used for an introduction? How is it effective?

- What is the twist in the conclusion? What idea is the reader left to think about after the essay is over?

☐ 2. Complete the **Prewriting Sheet: Connection Inspection**.

☐ 3. Using your Prewriting Sheet, write up a draft. You may want to start with your claim and write the intro last. Be sure that each paragraph has only one main idea with examples.

☐ 4. Cite your quotes. Your essay should be _____ page(s).

☐ 5. Be sure to have an engaging intro and a thought-provoking conclusion.

☐ 6. Read your draft and revise. Upgrade four verbs and add a title. Edit your work.

☐ 7. Submit your prewriting, drafts, final copy, and this sheet.

		Preliminary Grade	Revised Grade
Structure (length, paragraphs, title)	20%		
Process (prewriting, drafts, editing)	20%		
Ideas (claim, 1 main idea per paragraph, details, use of quotes, intro, conclusion)	20%		
Language (no banned words, clichés, wordiness; strong verbs, transition words)	20%		
Grammar/Spelling (punctuation, tenses, sentences, _____)	20%		
TOTAL			

Name _____ Date _____

Connection Inspection

1. Think of two works you can somehow connect. Here are some ideas:

    - Two separate works (poem, story, song, painting) that have a similar theme

    - A modern television show or movie with the same plot or theme as a book

    - A proverb that can apply to the characters of a story

    - Two characters from different works who have similar struggles and growth

    - The similarities and differences of a certain setting in two different works

    - A pattern of figurative language used by one author in different works

    Brainstorm a list of works you could connect. Circle the two you will write about in your essay.

2. Now, using the two works you circled above, brainstorm some ways they connect to each other. List as many as you can.

3. Look at the connections you brainstormed above, and choose three that would be interesting to explore in an essay. Resist using the most obvious ones. On the back of this page, map out your ideas, adding details.

4. When finished with the chart, ask yourself what main idea these connections suggest. How do they tie together? Write a sentence that encapsulates the overall idea of your connections on another sheet of paper.

5. What might be an engaging way to begin? (The intro could also be a good place to get some of the obvious points of connection out of the way.) List one or two intro techniques that could work on your paper.

6. How could you give a twist at the end? How could you leave the reader thinking? Brainstorm some conclusion techniques on your paper.

continued on next page

Connection Inspection—Examples and Evidence

Topic: _____

Connection Idea	Specific Example/Quote from Work	Page #
	Work 1: Work 2:	
	Work 1: Work 2:	
	Work 1: Work 2:	
	Work 1: Work 2:	

How to Access Online Resources

Go to www.scholastic.com/writing-for-higher-standards and enter your email address and this code: **SC811145**.

Resource Number	Name	See page
0	Mini-Lesson Topics	7
1	Life List Questions	9
2	Practice Paragraph: Identify and Rewrite Clichés	10
8.1	Expository/Persuasive-1 Editing Check Sheet	22
8.2	Expository/Persuasive-2 Editing Check Sheet	22
8.3	Narrative Editing Check Sheet	22
8.4	Analysis Editing Check Sheet	22
9.1	Writing Assignment: Setting Sketch	23
9.2	Prewriting Sheet: Setting Sketch	23
9.3	Model Writing: Setting Sketch	23
10.1	Writing Assignment: Character Sketch	24
10.2	Prewriting Questions: Character Sketch	24
10.3	Model Writing: Character Sketch	24
11.1	Writing Assignment: Free Verse Memory Poem	24
11.2	Prewriting Sheet: Free Verse Memory Poem	24
11.3	Model Writing: Free Verse Memory Poem	24
12.1	Writing Assignment: Autobiographical Incident	24
12.2	Prewriting Sheet: Autobiographical Incident	24
12.3	Prewriting Sheet: Short Story	24
12.4	Partner Interview: Autobiographical Incident	24
12.5	Model Writing: Autobiographical Incident	24
13.1	Writing Assignment: Proverb Story	24
13.2	Prewriting Sheet: Proverb Story	24
13.3	Model Writing: Proverb Story	24
13.4	Prewriting Sheet: Short Story	24
14.1	Writing Assignment: Retelling of a Legend	25
14.2	Prewriting Sheet: Retelling of a Legend	25
14.3	Model Writing: Retelling of a Legend	25
14.4	Prewriting Sheet: Short Story	25
15.1	Writing Assignment: Historical Ballad	25
15.2	Prewriting Sheet: Historical Ballad	25
15.3	Model Writing: Historical Ballad	25

Resource Number	Name	See page
16.1	Writing Assignment: Personal Ballad	25
16.2	Brainstorming Chart: Personal Ballad	25
16.3	Model Writing: Personal Ballad	25
17.1	Writing Assignment: Children's Book	25
17.2	Prewriting Sheet: Children's Book	25
17.3	Storyboard: Children's Book	25
18.1	Writing Assignment: Living Legend	26
18.2	Prewriting Sheet: Living Legend Interview	26
18.3	Model Writing: Living Legend	26
18.4	Prewriting Sheet: Short Story	26
19.1	Writing Assignment: Short Story	26
19.2	Prewriting Sheet: Short Story Concept	26
19.3	Prewriting Sheet: Short Story	26
19.4	Model Writing: Short Story	26
20.1	Writing Assignment: Historical Fiction	26
20.2	Research Sheet: Historical Fiction	26
20.3	Prewriting Sheet: Short Story Concept	26
20.4	Prewriting Sheet: Short Story	26
21	Writing Assignment: Introduce Yourself!	56
22.1	Writing Assignment: What's in a Name?	57
22.2	Prewriting Sheet: What's in a Name?	57
22.3	Model Writing: What's in a Name?	57
23.1	Writing Assignment: Me, in Metaphors	57
23.2	Prewriting Sheet: Me, in Metaphors	57
23.3	Model Writing: Me, in Metaphors	57
24.1	Writing Assignment: Epic Hero Shield and Reflection Part 1	57
24.2	Brainstorming Sheet: Epic Hero Shield	57
24.3	Writing Assignment: Epic Hero Shield and Reflection Part 2	57
25.1	Writing Assignment: Classify Your Crib	57
25.2	Prewriting Sheet: Classify Your Crib	57
26.1	Writing Assignment: Process Essay	58
26.2	Prewriting Sheet: Process Essay	58
26.3	Model Writing: Process Essay	58

Resource Number	Name	See page
27.1	Writing Assignment: Ode	
27.2	Prewriting Sheet: Ode	58
27.3	Model Writing: Ode	
28.1	Writing Assignment: Thank-You Letter	
28.2	Prewriting Sheet: Thank-You Letter	58
28.3	Model Writing: Thank-You Letter	
29.1	Writing Assignment: Compare and Contrast Essay	
29.2	Prewriting Sheet: Compare and Contrast Essay	58
29.3	T-Chart	
29.4	Model Writing: Compare & Contrast Essay	
30.1	Writing Assignment: Break Up With a Bad Habit	
30.2	Prewriting Sheet: Break Up With a Bad Habit	58
30.3	Model Writing: Break Up With a Bad Habit	
31.1	Writing Assignment: School Survival Guide	59
31.2	Prewriting Sheet: School Survival Guide	
32.1	Writing Assignment: News Account	59
32.2	Prewriting Sheet: News Account	
33.1	Writing Assignment: Passion Pursuit	59
33.2	Prewriting Sheet: Passion Pursuit	
34.1	Writing Assignment: Ponder the Progress	59
34.2	Prewriting Sheet: Ponder the Progress	
35.1	Writing Assignment: Travel Brochure	
35.2	Prewriting Sheet: Travel Brochure	88
35.3	Model Writing: Travel Brochure	
36.1	Writing Assignment: Product Review	89
36.2	Prewriting Sheet: Product Review	
37.1	Writing Assignment: Book Review	
37.2	Prewriting Sheet: Book Review	89
37.3	How to Have an Opinion About Literature	
38.1	Writing Assignment: Arts Review	
38.2	Prewriting Sheet: Arts Review	90
38.3	How to Have an Opinion About the Arts	
39.1	Writing Assignment: Parental Persuasion	
39.2	Prewriting Sheet: Parental Persuasion	90
39.3	Model Writing: Parental Persuasion	

Resource Number	Name	See page
40.1	Writing Assignment: Letter to the Principal	
40.2	Prewriting Sheet: Letter to the Principal	90
40.3	Idea Sheet: Letter to the Principal	
40.4	Model Writing: Letter to the Principal	
41.1	Writing Assignment: Letter for Social Change	
41.2	Prewriting Sheet: Letter for Social Change	90
41.3	Model Writing: Letter for Social Change	
42.1	Writing Assignment: Public Service Announcement	
42.2	Prewriting Sheet: Public Service Announcement	91
43.1	Writing Assignment: Personal Essay	
43.2	Prewriting Sheet: Personal Essay	91
43.3	Model Writing: Personal Essay	
44.1	Writing Assignment: Analysis of a Song	
44.2	Prewriting Sheet: Analysis of a Song	91
44.3	Model Writing: Analysis of a Song	
45.1	Writing Assignment: Analysis of a Poem	
45.2	Prewriting Sheet: Analysis of a Poem	92
45.3	Model Writing: Analysis of a Poem	
46.1	Writing Assignment: Analysis of Art	
46.2	Prewriting Sheet: Analysis of Art	92
46.3	Model Writing: Analysis of Art	
47.1	Writing Assignment: Analysis of a Character	
47.2	Prewriting Activity: Analysis of a Character	92
47.3	Model Writing: Analysis of a Character	
48.1	Writing Assignment: Analysis of a Short Story	
48.2	Prewriting Sheet: Analysis of a Short Story	93
48.3	Model Writing: Analysis of a Short Story	
49.1	Writing Assignment: Analysis of an Article	
49.2	Prewriting Sheet: Analysis of an Article	93
50.1	Writing Assignment: Connection Inspection	
50.2	Prewriting Sheet: Connection Inspection	93
50.3	Model Writing: Connection Inspection	